Hayer

D1326019

LOCAL HISTORY

OBJECTIVE AND PURSUIT

LOCAL HISTORY
OBJECTIVE AND PURSUIT

by

H. P. R. FINBERG
and
V. H. T. SKIPP

DAVID & CHARLES
NEWTON ABBOT

0 7153 4159 6

First published 1967
Second impression 1973

Printed in Great Britain
by W J Holman Limited Dawlish
For David & Charles (Holdings) Limited
South Devon House Newton Abbot Devon

CONTENTS

PREFACE

I T was the fascination of the subject, the continuous excitement of research, which first attracted me, as it has attracted many others, to
the pursuit of local history. The question "what is
the use of it?" did not trouble me, for any but the
most philistine view of man and the universe must
find room for some forms of intellectual activity
which are ends in themselves. Whether local history was one of them could hardly be decided until
its nature and aims were clarified; in the meantime,
if I engaged in it for my own recreation, as another
man might choose to play golf or go sailing, no
apology was called for, even to myself.

Many people are content to leave it at that. Not
long ago the Standing Conference for Local History, which brings together in membership repre-
sentative amateurs from all over the country,
devoted half a day at its annual meeting to a general
discussion of the question "What is local history?"
It proved entirely futile. The all but universal feeling seemed to be: "We don't know what we mean
by local history, and we don't care; but we mean to
go on with it."

Such enthusiasm commands respect, but would
it be any less dynamic if directed and informed by
a well-defined conception of the subject-matter? An
obstinately rationalistic bias left me discontented
with the vagueness in which the subject was en-
veloped, and anxious to make clear, if only to myself, what I was really doing, or trying to do. The
challenge became more urgent when an unexpected

chain of circumstances led me to apply for a vacant Readership which carried with it the headship of the unique Department of English Local History at the then University College of Leicester. The college was good enough to appoint me, and what had been a private hobby thus became a professional duty. Soon after taking up the post I was invited to deliver a public lecture on the subject. The first item reprinted in this book, a discourse on the Local Historian and his Theme, was the result. It elicited a leading article in the *Times Literary Supplement*, and continued to circulate in its original printed form throughout my tenure of the post at Leicester.

Some years later a firm of publishers invited me to compile and edit a symposium of historians, each of whom was to explain the *raison d'être*, as he understood it, of his own specialism. I took the opportunity to develop in more detail the thesis of the Leicester discourse. Later still, when the university thought fit to give me a chair, my inaugural lecture as the first Professor of English Local History was the obvious occasion for saying what I had to say about the place of the subject among academic disciplines.

At present it seems kinder to the reader, and more generally useful, to bring these occasional pieces together in one short book, and to explain the circumstances of their origin, than to attempt a more ambitious treatise on the theory and practice of local history. By way of light relief I include a hitherto unpublished lecture describing some of the pitfalls that await the novice.

During my stay at Leicester I dealt chiefly with individual students, men and women candidates for higher degrees, or who submitted written work for publication through one or other of the channels then at my disposal. It was no part of my duties to organize team-work in local history, or even to think much about it, though I was well aware that it was producing admirable results in various quarters under the leadership of devoted and able tutors. Fortunately one of the most successful practitioners in this field, Mr V. H. T. Skipp, has formulated his ideas in a paper which also gives an inspiring account of his own methods. There remain the schools, a domain into which local history is now penetrating far and wide; and here again Mr Skipp's remarks will be read with profit by all whom it concerns.

We hope this little collection will stimulate thought and discussion among students, teachers, and amateurs. All the indications point to a bright future for the local historian. As he pores over the tattered parchments or tramps the difficult miles, he needs—whether he knows it or not—some sort of guiding light. If he does not find it in these pages, they may at least provoke him to look further and discover one in his own deeper reflections.

H. P. R. FINBERG

THE LOCAL HISTORIAN AND HIS THEME

An Introductory Lecture
delivered at the University College of Leicester
6 November 1952

By H. P. R. Finberg

IN 1890 a writer in the *Saturday Review* expressed the opinion that "of all dull books a conscientiously compiled parochial history is the dullest." More recently an American scholar, engaged in collecting materials for a treatise on the English borough, found it necessary to consult a number of our local histories. He pronounced them to be mostly "so much dead weight on library shelves: vexatious to the student because of their disorderliness and wordiness; lacking most of what histories should contain, and containing much that histories should omit."[1]

So, on the threshold of the subject, we are greeted rather peevishly. And, it must be admitted, not without cause. Of the unnumbered books that have been written on the history of our counties, towns, and villages, few, if any, have been heard of by the general reader. There are no classics in this field, no local histories which are esteemed as masterpieces on a level with, say, Macaulay's *History of England*. Except when local piety, or the urgent curiosity of the professed student, blows off the accumulated

[1] M. de W. Hemmeon, *Burgage Tenure in Mediaeval England,* Cambridge (Mass.), 1914, p. 9.

dust, these folios, quartos, and octavos, fruits of so much devoted toil, are left unopened. Local history is the Cinderella among historical studies.

Nevertheless in recent years the universities have shown themselves disposed to take Cinderella under their protection. This may be just a counsel of despair; but I would rather construe it as an act of faith in the poor creature's possibilities. The first move was made as long ago as 1908, when, thanks mainly to private benefactions, a Research Fellowship in Local History was instituted at Reading. Despite the lustre conferred upon it by its first and only holder, F. M. Stenton, the post was discontinued after four years. In 1921 a Reader in the History of London was appointed at University College, London. Nine years later the University College of Hull set up a committee to promote research in the history of "the area more particularly served by the College": that is, the East Riding of Yorkshire and north Lincolnshire. Since 1949 there has been at the same college a staff Tutor in Local History; and by establishing, in the following year, a certificate in the subject, Hull again stood forth as one of Cinderella's doughtiest champions. In each case these developments occurred within the framework of existing departments: at London, in the department of history, and at Hull in that of adult education.[1] Only at the University College of Leicester has the subject as yet been accorded a department of its own. For this reason, and also because the department set up here in 1947 is not confined to any one area,

[1] I am indebted to the Registrars of Reading and Hull, and to the Secretary of University College, London, for the particulars given here.

but takes the local history of all England for its province, its establishment may be considered as a milestone in the progress of a new academic discipline.

While the younger academic bodies were taking these initiatives, and the senior universities were looking on indifferently, or perhaps averting their gaze in horror, Professor Arnold Toynbee was publishing the first instalments of his great treatise on world-history. That celebrated work might seem at first sight to have little direct bearing on my theme; but the propositions on which its argument is based do in fact constitute an excellent starting-point for a discussion of local history and its relationship with other branches of historical study. Toynbee maintains that historians have been occupying themselves too exclusively with the fortunes of the national state. He shows that the life of England, and still more obviously the lives of France, Germany, Spain, have been profoundly affected at all the crucial points by forces operating from outside the national frontiers. Consequently their history cannot be understood unless we study them as parts of a larger entity. The histories of England, France, and Spain are merely chapters in the history of Western Society as a whole. This greater society is "an intelligible field of study"; its component nations, taken by themselves, are not. Therefore historians will do well to "devote a larger share of their energy and acumen" to the study of Western Society and of the other great societies whose actions and interactions make up the sum of world-history.[1]

In urging this plea, Toynbee sometimes uses ex-

[1] Arnold J. Toynbee, *A Study of History*, Oxford, 1934– , I, pp. 17–50.

pressions which could be taken as implying that it is a waste of time to study national history. Nevertheless he would probably admit that it is normal and natural for Englishmen to take a particular interest in the history of England, and even to find it more readily intelligible than the history of other nations. For our part, we may agree with him that it cannot be fully understood in isolation from the supra-national entity of which England has formed a part. Our interest in the story of our own people does not spring only from natural sympathy: it can be fully justified on Toynbee's principles. For, as he himself points out, the national community is an "articulation" of the larger society to which it belongs; and while urging us "to think in terms of the whole and not of the parts," he observes that "different parts are differently affected by an identical general cause, because they each react, and each contribute, in a different way to the forces which that same cause sets in motion." We may put it in homelier terms: it takes all sorts to make a world. If every man were just like his neighbours, there would be no employment for the biographer; and it is because nations differ that each of them has a history of its own. Therefore we study the history of Western Christendom in order to grasp the unity of the member-nations, and we study the history of the nations in order to realize their diversity. As one of Stendhal's characters observes, the verisimilitude of a story lies wholly in the details.[1]

[1] "Vers le milieu du récit, M. Leuwen commença à faire des questions. 'Plus de détails, plus de détails,' disait-il à son fils, 'il n'y a d'originalité et de vérité que dans les détails.' "—*Lucien Leuwen*, 1926, iv, p. 169.

Now it seems to me that this argument can be extended and applied with equal force to small communities within the nation. Professor Toynbee, sweeping ecumenical horizons with his telescope, exhorts the student of history to brace himself for "mental operations on a larger scale." But the telescope, as others before me have remarked, is not the only instrument that will broaden our minds and enlarge the stock of knowledge: the microscope also has its uses. And within the nation there are smaller communities which have every right to be considered as distinct articulations of the national life. One can think of hundreds of rural and urban communities which have possessed a spiritual and economic vitality of their own, and their own organs of local government. It is true that such communities are not much in evidence today. A man who lived in London all his life might never have the idea of a local community brought home to his consciousness at all. You do not feel that you are crossing a frontier when you pass from the metropolitan borough of Paddington into the royal borough of Kensington. But if you go far enough afield, you can still find local consciousness asserting itself even now at something like its old strength. Last year I spent some time exploring the Forest of Dean. Lying between the Severn and the Wye, this district has well-marked natural limits; and its inhabitants are physically distinguishable from their neighbours. They belong to the county of Gloucester, but if you come from east of the Severn they will say you come from Gloucestershire, and if you come from some other county they will say quite simply that you are a foreigner. Their principal industry, the mining of coal and iron, has been carried on ever since the Roman period. The powers vested in the Coal Commission under the Act of 1938, to grant or refuse a lease of coal entirely at their discretion, operate in all the coalfields of Great Britain with the one exception of the Forest of Dean. Here the powers of the Commission are still subject to the rights and privileges of the Free Miners of the Hundred of St Briavels. The mine-court no longer meets, but the court of verderers still holds occasional sessions at the Speech House, built for the purpose in 1670. One man with whom I had some talk began his working life as a miner, then, becoming partly disabled, opened a garage and started a service of local buses. Presently one of the big bus companies offered to buy him out. He refused to sell; so the company tried to oust him by running two buses for every one of his, with one bus running five minutes ahead and the other five minutes behind him. But his customers were not going to let a Forest man be done down by a pack of *foreigners*; and in the end it was the company's buses that had to be withdrawn.

The commoners and Free Miners of Dean are today what the people of nearly every English town and rural district were until the day before yesterday: a self-conscious local community. And though it may be difficult for us to grasp the fact with our imaginations, it is nevertheless true that for centuries the local community provided the normal setting in which Tom, Dick, and Harry lived and worked and played. Their bread was made from corn grown under a communal system of agriculture in the soil of the parish, and ground at the local mill.

Their other material needs were supplied from the nearest market town, and their spiritual needs at the parish church or nowhere. They thought of themselves as Englishmen, certainly; but the abiding and ever-present reality was that they were inhabitants of Plumstead or Hogglestock or Barchester.

Each of these rural or urban communities has reacted and contributed in its own characteristic way to the main currents of English history. And note that it has done so in its own good time. For its life-span is not necessarily co-extensive with that of the nation as a whole. A local community may come into existence at almost any date, lead a more or less vigorous life of its own for a century or two, or for the better part of a millennium, and then fade out again, even as the republic of Venice and the empire of Austria have faded from the map of Western Christendom. Take for example the village of Whatborough, one of the oldest settlements in Leicestershire, established as far back perhaps as the sixth century, and so completely blotted out by the enclosure movement of the fourteen-nineties that an estate map drawn in 1586 has a blank space in the centre, inscribed: "The Place where the Town of Whatboroughe stood."[1] On the urban scale, Cheltenham, transformed in the second half of the eighteenth century from a rural market-centre into a fashionable spa, and Middlesbrough, down to 1831 a township of fewer than a hundred souls, now a great manufacturing city and an epis-

[1] R. H. Tawney, *The Agrarian Problem in the Sixteenth Century*, London, 1912, p. 223. "Town" here signifies a township, or rural community. See also *Studies in Leicestershire Agrarian History*, ed. W. G. Hoskins, Leicester, 1949, p. 96.

B

copal see, exemplify changes so drastic that we may
fairly call them new creations. In our own lifetime
we have seen local communities brought into being
ab ovo at Welwyn and elsewhere. Not only in these
organisms of recent growth, but in many a small
town and big provincial city there may be found,
even at this day, a strong civic spirit and a pride in
local achievement. But there is not the old degree of
social cohesion. A railwayman or a mill-owner today
pretty certainly feels himself more closely linked
in sympathies and interests and aspirations with his
fellow-railwaymen or fellow-manufacturers up and
down the country than with the majority of his fel-
low-townsmen. Moreover, Leviathan, as we all
know, looks with no friendly eye upon allegiances
that are not centred on its omnicompetent self. It
may be that just as the family, once so powerful a
unit, has withered into social impotence, so the local
community is destined to wither in its turn. But
while it flourished it yielded only to the nation, and
not always even to the nation, in its hold over men's
loyalties.[1]

As soon, however, as we propose to write its history, voices are raised in a shrill chorus of dissuasion.
Dr G. M. Trevelyan makes no secret of the light in
which he views the subject. He writes: "Ever since
the publication of *Tudor Cornwall* I have believed
that Mr A. L. Rowse had it in him to become an
historian of high rank if he would lay aside lesser

---

[1] A leading article has just appeared in *The Times* (27 August
1952) suggesting that measures should be taken to arrest the decay of our smaller and middle-sized country towns "in these days
when transport by bus has brought about revolutionary changes
in country habits."

activities and bend himself to the production of history on the grand scale."[1] So the dilemma confronts us in all its nakedness: if you write local history badly, you are the dreariest of bores; and if you write it as well as Mr Rowse, it is a pity you cannot find something better to do. Then there is Professor Toynbee, who will argue that if the history of England is not self-explanatory, *a fortiori* neither is the history of Barchester. And we readily agree that Barchester, taken by itself, is not a fully intelligible field of study. We know, for example, that the Latin mass, which had been offered in Barchester cathedral ever since the cathedral was built, ceased to be offered there in the sixteenth century for reasons which must be sought ultimately not in Barchester itself, nor even in London, but at Prague and Wittenberg and Rome. Even so, the course the Reformation took in Barchester was not that which it took in Stockholm or Amsterdam; and Barset, though more thoroughly 'reformed' than Lancashire, was perhaps a shade less so than the eastern counties. Thus Barchester stands out as a distinct articulation, not only of the national community, but of Western Society as a whole. And if so, its history is a field of study which deserves to be cultivated for its own sake.[2] To anyone who thinks it absurd that

[1] *Sunday Times*, reviewing *The England of Elizabeth*, vol. 1.

[2] As Professor Toynbee implicitly allows, when he declares that history, as a humane study, is properly concerned with the lives of societies in both their internal and their external aspects. "The internal aspect is the articulation of the life of any given society into a series of chapters succeeding one another in time and into a number of communities living side by side. The external aspect is the relation of particular societies with one another."—*op. cit.*, 1, p. 46.

we should labour day and night only to "chronicle small beer," let Chesterton's parable supply the answer. " 'Notting Hill,' said the Provost simply, 'is a rise or high ground of the common earth, on which men have built houses to live, in which they are born, fall in love, pray, marry, and die. Why should I think it absurd?' "

It may be objected that so many of our English local communities being now either dead or moribund, the historian would do better to concentrate on subjects of living interest. To this the obvious answer is that the Hellenic city-state and the empire of Rome are also dead, but we do not therefore consign them to oblivion. To the historian it may be a positive advantage that he is dealing with something which has finished its course. His ultimate function is to tell a story, and every story is more readable, more shapely, if it has an end as well as a beginning.

The business of the local historian, then, as I see it, is to re-enact in his own mind, and to portray for his readers, the Origin, Growth, Decline, and Fall of a Local Community. If this principle is accepted, it becomes possible to define with something like precision the relationship between his study and other disciplines, whether academic or non-academic. The sources he must consult will be part written, part unwritten. In so far as he deals with unwritten evidences, we may style him an archaeologist. He is also a geographer, since part of his task is to elucidate in detail the process of *défrichement*— we have no English word for it—whereby the soil of his parish has been subdued to human purposes by gradual conquest of the primeval marsh or woodland. He is not a geologist, but he interrogates the geologist on the character of the soil and the structure of the underlying rocks, because without this knowledge he cannot rightly interpret the effects of human action upon the landscape. His contribution to historical geography demands an intensive observation of fields, hedges, roads, and water-courses. Much of his time is thus spent out of doors; but since field-work must be controlled and amplified by documentary research, he is also an assiduous visitor at libraries, record offices, and muniment rooms. He is an economic historian because the greater part of man's life is spent in gaining a livelihood, and a historian of art and education and religion because man does not live by bread alone. Though he never, I hope, utters the fatuous word 'medieval', which has even less meaning for local than for national and ecumenical history, he is perforce a medievalist because the so-called Middle Ages were the formative period in the life of most English towns and villages, and indeed covered something like two-thirds of their whole existence. But he is also a modernist, if that is the right word, because many of them survived as local communities into the age of railways and motor transport. He is thus not a specialist in any one period; nor is his an antiquarian pursuit. Antiquary is a word of fluid meaning, but I take it to mean one who studies the monuments of antiquity—usually a single class of monument—for their own sakes. For the antiquarian the sculptures on the west front of Barchester cathedral, or the cross-legged effigies in the parish churches, are objects to be studied in relation to each other and to similar monuments elsewhere.

For the historian they are particular manifestations
or expressions of a social life which he is trying to
reconstruct in its entirety.

It is sometimes held that local history provides a
useful method of approach to national history. And
it is true that sometimes a train of momentous hap-
penings is found to have been touched off in some
village whose chronicler, by revealing this fact,
teaches the national historian something he might
not have discovered for himself. It is also true that
if the histories of all our parishes were written as
they should be written, the history of England
would need to be revised at many points. It may be,
also, that a teacher who wishes to give his pupils
something more than a 'notional apprehension' of
English history will find it helpful to illustrate the
Wars of the Roses by showing them the tomb of
Sir William in the parish church, or the strife of
Cavalier and Roundhead by pointing out the ruins
of Sir Lionel's mansion. But I am quite sure that to
esteem local history only or chiefly for its propae-
deutic value is to underestimate it, and that to treat
it as an introduction or a contribution to national
history is to invert the true relationship between
them. We may grant that the history of Meryton
or Mellstock will help us to understand the history
of England, just as the history of England will help
us to understand the history of Western Christendom; but it remains true that a study of the whole
will do more to enlighten us about any single part
than vice versa. In other words, when we are sufficiently familiar with the European past to read
English history intelligently, and when we are
thoroughly well grounded in the history of Eng-

land: then, and not till then, can we begin to think of writing the history of Liverpool or Lydiard Millicent or Saffron Walden. Local history is not an elementary study. It is one to which the amateur or the young student can, and often does, make a valuable contribution; but in its higher reaches it demands mature scholarship and a wide background of general culture.

Another claim that I will venture to make for it is that local history is pre-eminently a humane discipline. Let me recall here the well-known little rhyme:

> The art of biography
> Is different from geography.
> Geography is about maps,
> But biography is about chaps.

History too is "about chaps," and local history brings us nearer to the common run of chaps than any other branch of historical study. It gives us, in the language of the films, a close-up of them on their farms and in their workshops and behind their counters. It studies them as social beings, as members of a rural or urban community; but by seeking them at their home address it enables us to see them as flesh and blood, and not just as pawns on the national chessboard. The national historian, dealing with some vast agglomeration which he labels villeins, Puritans, the lower middle-class, or what you will, tends to lose sight of the human person.[1]

---

[1] "Even in the study of history a kind of acquired simplicity is needed just to see things as they really are, just to see things naked, instead of envisaging them in the categories which historians have created to fit them into—attributing things to the Renaissance

In the preface to *The Reign of Elizabeth*, one of the earliest published volumes of the Oxford History of England, the author, Professor J. B. Black, says: "In the present volume we have been compelled to observe events predominantly through English eyes, or, to be more correct, through the eyes of the English government." He goes on to remark that other points of view have an equally good claim to be considered, and says he has tried to bear this in mind, "but *the paramount necessity of placing the reader at the standpoint of the queen and her ministers* has prevented a rigorous following out of the principle."[1] We naturally wonder who laid this necessity upon him: was it the editor, or the delegates of the Clarendon Press? But no explanation is vouchsafed. If the reign of Elizabeth II had to be dealt with on this plan, I suppose one would begin to write its history from the standpoint of Mr Churchill, and if a general election should bring Mr Attlee into power, keep the printer working overtime to bring out a revised edition. For let us remember that the phrase "Her Majesty's Opposition" dates only from 1826; in the time of the first Elizabeth opposition was just a short cut to the scaffold. The standpoint of an angel, gazing with pity and comprehension at the antics of mortal men, is of course beyond our reach, but one can think of several purely human standpoints from which national history could be studied more intelligently than from that of the group which has contrived to make itself,

when the Renaissance is a mere label that historians have chosen to apply to a generation of people."—H. Butterfield, *Christianity and History*, London, 1949, p. 115.

[1] The italics are mine.

at a given moment, master of the state. Local history brings us face to face with the Englishman at home, and reminds us that it is he who foots the bill his rulers have run up for him. By so doing, it restrains the propensity to worship mere power and success, a propensity which loses none of its baseness from being carried back into our study of the past.

From time to time we seem to detect, in the making of national history, an element of downright imposture. Take for example the case of Richard Strode. Strode came of a Devonshire family seated at Newnham, in Plympton St Mary; and he represented the borough of Plympton in the parliament of 1512. He was also an owner or part-owner of tin-works. It appears that two partners, William Rede and Elis Elforde, started digging for tin on Strode's land. These two were jurors for Plympton at a Great Court of the Devon Stannaries which had just reaffirmed the right, guaranteed to all tinners by immemorial custom and by charter of Edward I, "to dig tin in every place within the county of Devonshire whereas tin may be found"; and the Great Court had decreed that any one obstructing this right should be liable to a fine of forty pounds. In order to rid himself of his unbidden guests without incurring the penalty appointed, Strode introduced a bill into the parliament of Westminster to restrain mining operations in the vicinity of seaports, alleging that the harbours of Devon were being choked with refuse from the mines. The bill, though it did not become law, aroused great indignation among the tinners; and at the next law-day the under-steward caused Strode to be presented at all four stannary courts for conduct subversive of the miners' liberties. The culprit was fined forty pounds in each court; but refusing to pay, was arrested "and imprysoned in a dongeon and a deepe pitte under the ground in the castel of Lidford . . . the which prison," as he afterwards feelingly declared, "is one of the most annoious, contagious, and detestable places wythin this realme." After languishing there for some three weeks, he was released by a writ of privilege from the Exchequer, not as a member of parliament, but as a collector of the subsidy that had just been voted to the Crown. Before releasing him, the deputy warden required him to give bail for one hundred pounds. To secure himself against forfeiture of bail and further pursuit, Strode now complained to parliament, and persuaded it to pass a statute not only annulling his condemnation in the stannary courts, but granting immunity to him and his associates for anything done or to be done by them in that or future parliaments.[1] It is important to note that the provisions of the act are limited to Strode himself "and every other of the person or persons afore specifyed": that is, those "other of this house" who had joined him in promoting a bill against the tinners. It was thus a particular, not a general statute; and the only question of principle involved was whether the legislative competence of parliament should or should not override that of a self-governing local body like the Stannaries. Neither the parliament which enacted it, nor Henry VIII who gave it his assent, had the least intention of making it a corner-stone of

[1] 4 Hen. VIII, c. 8. A schedule annexed to the act enables us to follow the affair in detail.

privilege. Both before and after the passing of Strode's act the sovereign claimed and sometimes exercised the right to punish members of the house of commons when they overstepped their constitutional function as voters of supply. But under the Stuarts this right became the subject of hot debate. The upholders of parliamentary immunity never shrank from using bad law and bogus history to support their claims;[1] and as one of the five members whom Charles I tried but failed to arrest was a lineal descendant of Richard Strode, the precedent of 1512 was not likely to be overlooked. Finally, in 1667, Lords and Commons, evidently persuaded that two and two make five if parliament will have it so, passed a joint resolution affirming the "Act concerning Richard Strode" to be "a general Law . . . declaratory . . . of the ancient and necessary Rights and Privileges of Parliament."[2] After this, it is not surprising to find even so eminent an authority as Halsbury censuring the Tudor and Stuart monarchs because they "chose to regard it" in a different light.[3]

It was said of the Leicester antiquary Thomas Staveley that "having passed the latter part of his

[1] Hence the interesting design of the Lord Keeper Francis North to print and publish "all the records of state and parliament," because he was convinced that such publication would help the monarchy against its adversaries.—*Lives of the Norths*, ed. Jessopp, 1890, I, p. 355.

[2] *Journals of the House of Lords*, XII, p. 166. The Commons admitted that the statute was made "upon a private and particular Occasion"; but in the teeth of history, and by a plain misreading of the text, they asserted that it was meant to cover "all Members that then were, or ever should be."

[3] *The Laws of England*, London, 1907–17, XXI, p. 782.

life in the study of English history, he acquired a melancholy habit."[1] And when we consider the spirit in which our national history has all too frequently been written, we can understand the poor man's feelings. We may liken English history to a dish cooked in a vast kitchen, where the smoking fat of nineteenth-century liberalism mingles with the stale cabbage of Elizabethan no-popery propaganda and with a hundred other odours, new and old. But with local history we can escape, if we choose, into the fresh air. One cannot hope to establish a thesis of general application by writing the history of a parish, as Macaulay, for example, nearly succeeded in establishing the Whig thesis by writing a history of England. Therefore there is the less temptation to indulge in generalized passions for or against the various 'isms—feudalism, Protestantism, capitalism, and the rest. By setting us face to face with flesh and blood, local history puts a curb on those abstract hatreds which can so easily turn the heart to stone. For instance, you may hold that popery deserves the worst that has ever been said of it, and yet find it comparatively easy to acknowledge that the priest whom Burghley's police caught saying mass up at the manor-house, and who paid for it with his blood at Tyburn, was a not wholly despicable character. You may execrate the landed gentry and everything they stand for, and yet freely recognize that the present squire's grandfather was adored by his tenants and reared the finest herd of Ayrshires in the county. I am far from contending that local history will furnish us with any automatic-

[1] John Nichols, *History and Antiquities of the County of Leicester*, 1795–1815, II, p. 677.

ally effective antidote against partisanship. The local historian, like other men, will have his personal preferences and prepossessions. But if the milk of human kindness is not dried up within him, some fellow-feeling with "Hodge and his masters" will arise, even when he deems their conduct most perverse. You cannot paint a miniature with great splashes of blood-red.

The reasons why so many of the older local histories fail to satisfy us are now clear. The writers were content to heap up all the facts they could discover, without order, art, or method, and with no criterion for distinguishing the trivial from the significant. Their theme, if they can be said to have had a theme, was not the rise and fall of a local community, but the fortunes of one or two armigerous families. In this respect they had a perfect, if unconscious, spokesman in the late Sir George Sitwell. Mr Evelyn Waugh tells us that he was standing one evening, with other guests, on the terrace of Sir George's mansion at Renishaw. "In the valley at our feet . . . lay farms, cottages, villas, the railway, the colliery, and the densely teeming streets of the men who worked there . . . Sir George turned and spoke in the wistful, nostalgic tones of a castaway, yet of a castaway who was reconciled to his solitude. 'You see,' he said, 'there is *no one* between us and the Locker-Lampsons.' "[1] Many of the older local histories were written by country gentlemen of scholarly tastes like Sir George Sitwell, or by the parsons whom they had presented to their livings; and they reflect the interests of that class. Page after

[1] Osbert Sitwell, *Laughter in the Next Room*, London, 1949, p. 349.

page is filled with details concerning the successive families who have been lords of the manor. Few subjects are more tedious, yet to this day the descent of the manor occupies a quite inordinate amount of space in the Victoria County Histories; and at the end one is left with the impression that nobody ever lived in the parish but the squire and his relations. In this particular, and in some others, the Victoria County Histories, planned as they were over half a century ago, must be said to embody a conception of local history which is now largely obsolete.[1] I do not mean to imply that the squire either can or should be left out of the picture. On the contrary, one of the most important questions the historian should try to answer is how far the element of lordship is fundamental in the make-up of the local community. But though genealogy, family history, is a perfectly legitimate branch of study, it is but one of many which the local historian will lay under contribution if he has taken the full measure of his task.

History, as we all know, is a Greek word meaning enquiry. Multifarious are the questions the local historian will put to himself as he tramps the field-paths or scrutinizes antique parchments. Of what condition were the men who founded his community? Were they veterans of an Anglo-Saxon war-band, maintaining themselves chiefly by the labour of the conquered Britons, or free peasants brought over to fill homesteads from which the de-

[1] A welcome announcement by Mr R. B. Pugh, editor-in-chief of the Victoria County Histories, has just appeared (see *The Amateur Historian*, 1, 1952, p. 4). It foreshadows changes of emphasis and treatment which will go far to obviate the criticism levelled at the older volumes.

feated race had fled? What nucleus of cultivation did they find awaiting them? By what stages did their descendants enlarge their holdings at the expense of the surrounding marsh or woodland? What considerations guided the marking out of the manor and parish boundaries? When was the borough carved out of the manor, and for what purpose? At what date was the communal system of agriculture superseded by enclosures, and why not earlier or later? How successfully has the community withstood, from century to century, the vicissitudes of population and trade? In what degree have religious differences contributed since the sixteenth century to its disruption? Has the acceleration of transport in the last hundred years prolonged its life or hastened its decay?

Some of these questions may prove to be unanswerable. When the historian has done his best with the remainder, and with the hundred others that arise, let him muster every ounce of narrative and expository skill that he possesses, and begin to tell his tale. He may be confident that an audience will not be lacking. For as the older "glories of our blood and state" begin to wane, and the social revolution of the twentieth century brings in a new order which not all men find congenial, many of our fellow-countrymen are filled with a deeper curiosity than ever before concerning the old market towns of England: Stamford, Ludlow, Chipping Campden—the very names are music; and the beloved villages: Castle Combe, Colly Weston, Finchingfield: all those places which embody, in varying degrees of perfection, a social life that is fast vanishing, if it has not already gone; and they are eager to hear what the historian can tell them about that life, if only he can set forth an intelligible tale.

The local historian today starts out with one great advantage over his predecessors. With all their zeal and erudition, the writers of the old school lacked a central unifying theme. At their best they produced fine works of reference, but rarely a book that could be read from cover to cover with pleasure as well as profit. Today, with a much vaster and more accessible range of materials to draw upon, the scholar who sets out to trace the history of a rural or urban community has but to keep this theme steadily in view, and every fact that he uncovers will fall into place. His narrative will take shape as a block of marble takes shape under the sculptor's chisel.

If the ideas I have tried to develop here meet with approval, they may fitly serve as guiding principles for the conduct of the department which the University College of Leicester has entrusted to my care. Indeed, they may be said to have shaped its course already under my predecessor. The "new school"—as Mr Rowse termed it in a recent broadcast—has produced no historian more widely and justly admired than W. G. Hoskins. His books and lectures are at once learned, graphic, and humane. As first Reader in English Local History he set an example which may well inspire a feeling of diffidence in his successor, particularly a successor who has spent much of his working life in other fields. But his writings, and the discussions I have had with him at various times, lead me to believe that Dr Hoskins takes a view of local history which differs only in detail from mine. It is good to know also

that the department which occupies itself with national and international history has, in Professor
Simmons, a head keenly alive to the value of local
history. Finally, I take some courage from a back-
ward glance at three great amateurs in whose performance there was nothing amateurish. First, John
Nichols (1746–1826), to whose enthusiasm we are
mainly indebted for that grandest of record-publi-
cations, the folio edition of Domesday Book (1783),
and who, after publishing five volumes on *The History and Antiquities of the County of Leicester* at a loss
of as many thousand pounds, went on undismayed
and completed one of the finest of the older county
histories by publishing three more. Then his son,
John Bowyer Nichols (1779–1863), who super-
intended the publication of Ormerod's *Cheshire*,
Baker's *Northamptonshire*, Hoare's *Wiltshire*, and a
long list of other topographical master-works; and
his grandson, John Gough Nichols (1806–73), who
helped to found the Camden Society and edited
many of its publications. Few, if any, families have
done more to advance historical knowledge; and I
find it inspiriting to recollect that they accomplished
so much while carrying on their day-to-day business
as printers and publishers: trades which it has been
my fortune also to ply.

The primary aim of the department, then, will be
to foster, in our own minds and in the minds of any
who look to us for guidance, a reasoned conception
of local history, such as will set a standard of performance by which our work and the work of others
may be judged. That conception will oblige us to
demand, from ourselves and others, exact scholarship, wide sympathies, and a style of writing at once

C

precise and vivid. We must persuade scholars that no perfection of attainment is out of place in local history; that there is room here for a Maitland's brilliantly directed curiosity, for a command of documentary materials equal to that of Stubbs or Round, and for a narrative art comparable with the art of Green or Froude. And we must convince the public at large, not that local history is a fascinating subject, for the public is aware of that already, but that scholars have at last taught themselves how to unfold its true significance. If we can do this, the coming generation will be measurably nearer to producing the classic histories of our English towns and villages that are waiting to be written.

It is with these resolves, and with a feeling of deep gratitude to the College for giving me the opportunity to act upon them, that I take up my appointed task.

LOCAL HISTORY

By H. P. R. Finberg

I N 1908 the Board of Education issued a notable
circular on the teaching of history in secondary
schools. Notable because it appears to have been
the earliest state paper to accord local history a place
in the national system of education. For centuries
local history had been a favourite pursuit of elderly
antiquarians, but now it was to be pressed into service for the instruction of the young. "It is essential," said the Board, "that in each school attention
should be paid to the history of the town and district
in which it is situated."[1]

This pronouncement did not come quite as a bolt
from the blue. It had been preceded, and in all prob-
ability inspired, by a meeting of the Historical
Association, at which one speaker after another had
supported a plea for the teaching of local history in
schools. Their advocacy, however, stopped well
short of a disinterested and full-blooded enthusiasm
for the subject. "Of course we all agree," said Professor Hearnshaw—and only one of the speakers
who followed him did not agree—"that local history
must be used in a way entirely subsidiary." Subsidiary, that is, to the teaching of national history.
The young must not be encouraged to flounder
in "the bogs and sands of local detail," but they
might find history tedious if their lessons were not
enlivened by frequent references to things they

[1] Board of Education Circular 599, dated 25 November 1908,
p. 5.

could see around them or near their homes. "A lamp for the guidance and entertainment of the learner:" such was the function of local history according to its leading advocate, and elsewhere in his address he described it as "a storehouse of vivid and pregnant illustrations of the general course of national history."[1] This limited conception of its range was officially adopted by the Board of Education in the circular already quoted. The Board did not ask for separate courses of instruction in local history: all it required of teachers was that they should make "constant reference to the history of the locality as illustrative of the general history."

Thus local history makes its modest entry into the schools as "the sugar on the unpalatable but necessary pill that has to be administered to the young."[2] A parallel may be found in the use that great historians have made of local colour: one recalls, for instance, how Macaulay beguiles his readers with a graphic evocation of nineteenth-century Torquay, contrasting its "crowded marts" and "luxurious pavilions" with the naked shore that William of Orange approached in 1688. It is not at all surprising that the sugared pill should have found favour with the teaching profession. A teacher at

[1] Historical Association Leaflet No. 11, March 1908. The speaker was W. M. Childs, principal of what was then the University College of Reading. Some years later he justly claimed some credit for having promoted at Reading a living interest in the study of local history "as a means of illustrating the wider study of national history." From 1908 to 1912 the college possessed a research fellowship in local history, the first post of its kind in any English university, and memorable not only as such but as having been held by F. M. Stenton.

[2] Eric C. Walker, *History Teaching for To-day*, 1935, p. 96.

Battle, in Sussex, let us say, would be well placed for making his pupils understand the Norman Conquest: he could show them the hill up which the Normans charged, the very spot where Harold stood. By so doing, he would transform their merely notional apprehension of the conquest into a picture of real people and familiar scenes. The remains of Battle Abbey would also illustrate the doings of Henry VIII in at least one important aspect. On the other hand, if the teacher wished to speak of Magna Carta or the Reform Act, he might not find much illustrative material in Battle. As a mirror of the national history, almost any village or town one cares to name is likely to be incomplete. "Certain limitations must be admitted; it is no use looking to Derbyshire, an inland county, for illustrations of Elizabethan maritime enterprise which belongs properly to the West Country. And although Derbyshire offers some of the most tragic incidents of Mary Queen of Scots' life, little of importance will be found there about the Wars of the Roses or the pretenders of Henry VII's reign." These admissions, it will be noted, are made by a teacher who is prepared to ransack a whole county for his illustrations.[1]

From a different point of view the same preoccupation with national history was expressed some years ago when Dr G. M. Trevelyan represented local history as a sort of little harbour-boat in which a man is to find his sea-legs before launching out on the broad ocean of national history.[2] It is a training ground for historians of high rank, and as soon as they have acquired some proficiency they are en-

[1] *Ibid.*, p. 131.   [2] p. 9 above.

couraged to sally forth in search of better worlds to conquer. Against this notion scores of local antiquaries rise from their graves to protest, admirable and devoted scholars, many of them, whose highest ambition was to erect a worthy memorial of their own parish, town, or county.

Some of these learned men would conceivably have welcomed the definition of their undertaking propounded not long ago by Mr R. B. Pugh. In Mr Pugh's eyes local history is not just a sugared pill for young learners, nor a gymnasium in which promising historians may develop their muscles; it is a specialized technique of historical research. He defines it as "a method of ascertaining certain facts about the history of England by the minute examination of those areas smaller than the realm that combine to make the realm." In the same paragraph he likens it to the proceeding of the scientist who studies natural phenomena through a microscope.[1] Parcelling up the map of England into conveniently small administrative or topographical units, the local historian focuses attention on one of them in the hope of discovering new facts, or new light on old facts, and thereby enriching the history of England as a whole. In much the same way, the archaeologist who excavates a particular Roman villa hopes to enlarge our knowledge of Roman Britain.

Now it is certainly true that if the story of every parish in England could be told in full, we should know much more about the English past than we do; but the aggregate would still not be a history of England. That is not what Mr Pugh contends; he would almost certainly agree that in this case the

[1] R. B. Pugh, *How to write a Parish History*, 1954, p. 9.

whole is something other than the sum of its parts. He means, I take it, that all national histories are perforce written selectively. Faced with countless phenomena, the historian must bring them as best he can into manageable compass. He therefore selects those which impress him as significant, and arranges them into some sort of pattern. In doing so, he runs the risk of overlooking some local occurrence which, once perceived, necessarily upsets or alters the whole pattern. (Some years ago, if I may illustrate the point from my own experience, I investigated a dispute which revolved around an obscure village in east Devon. By so doing, I learnt more about the genesis of the civil war in Stephen's reign than could be gathered from all the standard histories put together.[1]) Again, the historian's choice of significant facts will be dictated as often as not by his own predilections. He may write as a partisan or propagandist; or—what very often comes to the same thing—he will tell the whole tale from the standpoint of the central government. Yet things seen from Westminster have a way of looking very different in the provinces. As the latest historian of High Wycombe has remarked: "We are in danger of falsifying history if we fail to realize that for the people of places like Wycombe their own borough was still the foreground of their view of the world, even in times of great national crisis."[2] The local historian, on the other hand, with his feet planted firmly on the ground, has a clearer and truer view, within his limited horizon, than the national his-

[1] H. P. R. Finberg, *Lucerna*, 1964, pp. 204–21.

[2] L. J. Ashford, *The History of the Borough of High Wycombe from its Origins to* 1880, 1960, p. 119.

torian surveying a vast field from his elevated watch-tower. He may supply important information which his more exalted colleague has overlooked; at the very least he provides a useful corrective, by exhibiting in all its diversity a past too complex to be securely imprisoned in generalized statements.

All this is true, and it will be seen that Mr Pugh gives local history a rather more dignified position among historical studies than the other writers I have quoted. But his ideas and theirs have one characteristic in common: an over-riding concern with national history. This is not surprising in an age like the present. We who enjoy the somewhat expensive privilege of living in the twentieth century inevitably find the national state looming large in our thoughts. Even when it is not plunging us into total war, it pursues, controls, and threatens us at every turn, taking toll of all our pleasures, saddling us with a burden of debt that we can never shake off, and, when we die, confiscating a handsome slice of anything we leave behind. But while none of us can forget it for a moment, the historian at least should be on his guard against permitting it to become an obsession. For, seen in historical perspective, any existing national state, our own included, is a thing of yesterday; and will anybody looking round the world we live in venture to prophesy that it still has a long life in front of it? To quote an American historian: "We are approaching the end of one of the great epochs of human history and the beginning of another. The period which is ending has lasted somewhat more than four centuries. It may be called the era of great national states. . . . In military, diplomatic, and some political aspects it may still be proper to think of Europe chiefly as a system of great national states. But in nearly every other aspect it is plain that the Age of Nations is approaching its end. The nation is ceasing to be the leading form of the world's structure; organizations transcending national boundaries are becoming more and more numerous and effective."[1] This was written as long ago as 1912, and nothing that has happened since diminishes its force.

Here is one form of bias, then, which the historian should try to correct. It is often an instinctive bias, born of natural affection for the land of one's birth. When one thinks of *King Lear*, and *Tom Jones*, and *Pride and Prejudice*, and the chapter-house at Wells, and Habeas Corpus, and Stilton cheese, and Cox's Orange Pippins, one may well feel glad to have been born in England; but neither this feeling nor the less agreeable attentions of the income-tax collector should blind us to the fact that other societies, both smaller and larger than the community of the realm, have had life-histories of their own. National history occupies an intermediate position between local and what for want of a better word may be called ecumenical history. Hence anyone who treats it as the be-all and end-all of historical study finds himself under fire today from two directions. On the one flank are the critics who contend, quite rightly, that the history of this country makes very little sense unless the narrator constantly depicts England as part of a larger whole. On the other side we hear what has been called the "Leicester school" of historians declaring that smaller communities than the

[1] J. Franklin Jackson, 'The Future Uses of History', reprinted in the *American Historical Review*, LXV, 1959, pp. 61–71.

nation, local communities, have a history which deserves to be studied for its own sake.[1]

We approach here a conception which differs
radically from those examined so far, in that it treats
local history not as an ancillary discipline but as one
subsisting in its own right. Those who take up this
position—and without more ado let me avow that I
am one of them—draw a distinction between local
history *per se* and national history localized. The
latter is what Mr Pugh seems to have in mind when
he speaks of "areas smaller than the realm that combine to make the realm" and recommends their
study as "a method of ascertaining certain facts
about the history of England." (Mr Pugh is editor-
in-chief of the Victoria County Histories; does he
really consider the six-score volumes of that massive
work to be nothing more than a footnote to somebody's yet unwritten History of England?) The
"Leicester school," on the other hand, insists that
the local historian should concern himself not with
areas as such, but with social entities. It declares
that his business is "to re-enact in his own mind, and
to portray for his readers, the Origin, Growth, Decline, and Fall of a Local Community."[2]

What do we mean here by 'community'? An
American scholar who examined ninety-four defini-

[1] The term "Leicester school" was first used by Professor Asa
Briggs when discussing work published by past and present members of the department of English Local History in the university
of Leicester.—*The New Statesman*, 15 February 1958.

[2] H. P. R. Finberg, *The Local Historian and his Theme*, reprinted *supra*, pp. 1–24. The same idea was propounded almost
simultaneously by Dr W. G. Hoskins in *History Today*, II, 1952,
p. 490.

tions of the term found that they agreed on only one point: namely, that it was something to do with human beings.[1] But his enquiry was conducted in a sociological context; for historical purposes the idea need not perplex us. Let us say that a community is a set of people occupying an area with defined territorial limits and so far united in thought and action as to feel a sense of belonging together, in contradistinction from the many outsiders who do not belong. This definition obviously fits the national community. It also fits, or has fitted in the past, many a smaller social aggregate, both rural and urban. True, on most men's lips today the word *foreigner* means a citizen of another country, but historically it means any outsider, a man from another town or from the next village. An incident recorded in 1833 illustrates vividly, though not in the most pleasing light, the exclusive spirit which formerly animated two market towns in Devonshire barely fifteen miles apart. A tipsy carter on his way back from Okehampton to Tavistock tried to ford the river instead of crossing the bridge. The day was stormy, and he soon found himself in extreme danger from one of the sudden swells to which the moorland streams are subject. Jumping from his horse on to a large rock that still kept its head above water, he called out for help. A passer-by fetched a rope, but finding it impossible to throw it far enough, he asked a couple of Okehampton men who came up to lend a hand. But after taking a good look at the carter, one of them said: " 'Tis a Tav-

[1] George A. Hillery, 'Definitions of Community', *Rural Soci ology*, xx, 1955, pp. 111–23.

'stock man; let un go." So they let him go, and the man of Tavistock was drowned.[1]

It would not be hard to find instances of similar antagonism between rural communities. In 1439 it was decreed that the men of Isleworth in Middlesex should beat the bounds of their parish on Monday or Tuesday in Rogation week, and their neighbours of Twickenham on the Wednesday, experience having shown that if the processions took place on the same day they usually ended in bloodshed.[2] On the other hand, there have been striking instances of co-operation between neighbouring communities. Describing the process by which nearly a hundred square miles were reclaimed from the Lincolnshire fens during the twelfth and thirteenth centuries, Dr Hallam observes: "Most of this reclamation was a communal process . . . the co-operation of comparatively free communities amongst themselves."[3] Again, the Cinque Ports acted with complete unanimity in their long-drawn struggle to retain control of the East Anglian herring trade, though here, it is true, the enemy was the 'foreign' borough of Yarmouth.[4] Even a shire could feel and act as a self-conscious unit. In 1313 "the community of the whole county" of Kent made petition to the justices in eyre "that they might be allowed

[1] Mrs Bray, *A Description of the Part of Devonshire bordering on the Tamar and the Tavy*, 1836, III, p. 170.

[2] M. Robbins, *Middlesex*, 1953, p. 303.

[3] H. E. Hallam, *The New Lands of Elloe*, Leicester University Press, 1954, p. 42.

[4] The Scottish boroughs appear to have shown a much greater capacity for united action than English boroughs in general; see T. Pagan, *The Convention of the Royal Burghs of Scotland*, Glasgow, 1926.

their customs which they had ever been used to have," customs, they said, "which were not in accordance with the common law." And the justices answered that the king would not have their customs taken away from them, but they had better put them in writing.[1]

Many and various have been the factors making for the cohesion of the local community. One of the most powerful, before the religious upheavals of the sixteenth and seventeenth centuries, was the unity of belief and worship that found its rallying-point in the parish church. For some time after that unity broke down, the young of all ranks continued to learn their letters at the local grammar school. On the secular side, fealty to the lord of the manor provided the community with a recognized head; and his court served as the local organ of justice and administration. In the borough craft guilds and merchant guilds looked after the townsmen's economic interests. The earliest formal grant of incorporation, that of Coventry in 1345, empowers the burgesses thenceforth to have "communitatem inter se," a community amongst themselves. Outside the boroughs thousands of villages and hamlets depended for their bread, meat, and ale on the sustained co-operation of common-field husbandry.

Few of these things, it must be allowed, are in evidence today. We have moved away from a world of small, intensely self-conscious local units into the world of megalopolis, or what the town-planner calls conurbations. Hence we are in danger of forgetting something which has played an immense part in the social experience of mankind. It may be difficult for

[1] Selden Society, xxiv, pp. 11, 18, 50.

us to conjure up a picture of the largely self-contained local community in the fullness of its life and vigour, but the measure of our difficulty is also the measure of our need to have its history put on record, for unless that is done a large and important tract of human experience will have passed beyond our ken.

It should be noted that the theme proposed here for local history possesses a time-scheme or chronology of its own, distinct from that of national history. For, leaving on one side the possibility that some of our towns and villages may have had a continuous existence from a Roman-British or a still more ancient starting-point, it is undeniable that many of them are older than the realm; they date, that is to say, from a time long before the kings of Wessex established a united English monarchy. On the other hand, there have been casualties. Quite a number of settlements recorded in Domesday Book vanished from the map a century or two later, and the enclosures of the fifteenth and sixteenth centuries wiped out hundreds more. Then there are the little market towns which from their date of origin in the twelfth or thirteenth century down to the era of stage-coaches flourished more or less vigorously, then perhaps resisted all too successfully the coming of the railway, became backwaters, and sank into a death-like trance, from which the later advent of motor transport may or may not have reawakened them. To counterbalance these losses there have been new births: eighteenth-century spas like Cheltenham, nineteenth-century railway towns like Swindon, twentieth-century 'garden cities'.

Thus the subject-matter of local history, as understood by the Leicester school, is not identical either in space or time with the subject-matter of national history. It follows that these are two different studies: the one is not a part of the other. The history of Mellstock or Barchester is not a mere fragment splintered off from the history of England: it deals with a social entity which has a perfectly good claim to be studied for its own sake.

To overthrow this claim, it would be necessary to establish one or other of three propositions. The opponent should convince us that the history of the English local community has been sufficiently well studied already; or that it is not worth studying; or that it cannot be studied at all. But when Mr Pugh writes: "English local history . . . is not or ought not to be an end in itself;" when Professor David Douglas, from the presidential chair of the Bristol and Gloucestershire Archaeological Society, assures his hearers that the distinction sometimes made [!] be-between what he calls general (meaning national) and local history is "completely arbitrary," and not only arbitrary but "meaningless,"[1] they are not arguing against the Leicester thesis: they are just ignoring it. The only writer who has condescended to argue the matter is Mr W. R. Powell, who recently propounded three objections.[2] In the first place, he says, rural and urban communities survive to this day all over England; it is therefore premature to speak of their decline and fall. Secondly, England from Saxon times to the present day has been an administrative unity, and "the actions of

[1] R. B. Pugh, *loc. cit.*; *Transactions of the B. and G. Arch. Soc.*, LXXVI, 1957, pp. 19, 20.
[2] W. R. Powell, 'Local History in Theory and Practice', *Bulletin of the Institute of Historical Research*, XXXI, 1958, pp. 41–8.

the central government have influenced the lives of people living in all parts of the country," so that the local community cannot usefully be studied in isolation. Thirdly, "in some, perhaps many, cases the story of the community can never be told, because the essential records are missing." Are we then to confine our attention to those communities which have left abundant records, and ignore the rest?

Before considering these objections, it is pertinent to enquire what Mr Powell understands by a local community. "No human community," he says, "can be truly said to have disintegrated while it includes people who are born, go to school, work, play, make love, worship, and die." This seems to land us back again in the sociological quagmire where the only thing that can be safely predicated of a community is that it consists of human beings. It is obvious that Mr Powell is not really envisaging anything like the closely integrated social formation which has been an ever-present, not to say obsessive, reality for so many thousands of people through the centuries.

In any case, the first objection rests on a misunderstanding. When we define the local historian's theme as embracing not only the origin and growth of a local community, but also its decline and fall, we are defining the theme at its fullest possible extension. We are not asking the historian to wait until a given community is dead before writing its history, any more than we are saying that nobody should write a history of England because England is not finished yet. "Origin and growth" may well be a sufficient and satisfying theme. Some even closer limitation of period can be accepted without the least demur. We are not saying no to the writer who should offer us a finely executed history of Elizabethan Ipswich or Georgian Weymouth or Victorian Exeter.

The second objection is identical with the reason Professor Douglas gave for his peremptory denial of independence to the local historian, namely, that he "can only make his work of general value if he constantly remembers that it is part of a larger whole." But if the local historian needs this reminder, so too does the national historian. What sense will the history of England make unless the narrator constantly remembers that England was once part of a united Western Christendom and is today a member of the Atlantic power-*bloc*? To recognize this, however, is not to admit that the history of England has no significance except as a chapter in the history of Europe. We may picture the family, the local community, the national state, and the supra-national society as a series of concentric circles. Each requires to be studied with constant reference to the one outside it; but the inner rings are not the less perfect circles for being wholly surrounded and enclosed by the outer.

The objection that for many local communities the "essential records" may be missing makes one wonder what records or class of records Mr Powell regards as essential. The smallest village has a name; so have its farms and fields; and modern place-name study has shown how much can be learnt about the pattern of early settlement from this source. The geological and geographical data are never missing. The church and perhaps other buildings will contribute their testimony. Nor are written records

D

likely to be wholly lacking. There will usually be an entry in Domesday Book; later, there will be parish registers, tax assessments, lawsuits; later still, census returns, directories, and newspapers. The sum-total of these materials may not produce a book of three hundred pages, but then not every community deserves or requires such extended treatment. The intrinsic interest of the theme, as well as the availability of materials, will dictate the proportions to be observed.[1] In any case, it will be time to consider what the local historian shall do next when the classic histories of our towns and villages have been written. At present all but a very few of them are still to come.

There are towns which, despite their modest size, have exhibited in a state of high perfection the most characteristic elements of our economic, religious, parliamentary, and civic history. A market-centre founded perhaps in the twelfth century on the domain of some bishopric or abbey, secularized three hundred years later, sending one or more representatives to parliament from the reign of Edward I to the Reform Act, experiencing the full force of the religious upheaval in the sixteenth century and of the subsequent divisions between church and chapel, struggling more or less successfully for municipal autonomy, earning its livelihood in twenty or a hundred different ways, and all the while preserving an ethos of its own, marked enough to

[1] For an excellent account of a community which never contained more than a dozen households, see M. F. Howson, 'Aughton, near Lancaster', in *Trans. Lancs. and Cheshire Antiquarian Soc.*, LXIX, 1959, pp. 15–42; and for one of an average Leicester village, W. G. Hoskins, *The Midland Peasant*, 1957.

differentiate it from towns which have passed through similar vicissitudes elsewhere: an urban community of this sort will present its would-be historian with an exacting and variegated theme, by no means lacking in drama. So too, in perhaps a quieter strain, will the rural community which from a date of origin far back in the Old English period to the age of parliamentary enclosure tilled its common fields, worshipped in its parish church untroubled by dissenting murmurs until the disciples of Wycliffe or Fox or Wesley broke up its unity of belief, and accepted more or less contentedly the dominance of a manorial lord until modern taxation drove the squire from his ancestral home. If these are to some extent typical patterns, we have also, by way of contrast, communities with eccentric, highly individual records: Barrow-in-Furness, for example, a new industrial town which the local bishop described in 1872 as being "one of the miracles of our time;" Stourport, the almost accidental offspring of a canal; or, again, Cleethorpes, where a poverty-stricken group of oyster-fishers, converted to Methodism by a follower of Wesley, was almost immediately transformed by the vogue for sea-bathing into a community of well-to-do boarding-house keepers, without abating one jot of its Methodism.

The theme, then, need not be dull, and for the student of humanity is certainly not insignificant. If the historian is to do it justice, what equipment must he possess?

In the first place, he should have a sufficient working knowledge of national and even international history, for we have agreed that the local community, even at its strongest, is subject to the most various

external pressures, and its history cannot be understood without reference to them. In other words, the
local historian must be at once a good Englishman
and a good European. Nor can he safely close his
eyes to the history of local communities other than
his own, for without some knowledge of them he
will be incapable of recognizing the distinctive features of the tale he sets out to unfold. We are requir-
ing him to be well read in more than one branch of
historical literature.

Next, let us wish him a lively topographical sense.
Gone for ever, let us hope, are the days when a man
could suppose it possible to write local history without ever stirring outside libraries and muniment-
rooms. A pair of legs not easily tired, an observant
eye, some acquaintance with geology and architecture, are necessary items of the equipment. For
every community will have left traces of its history
on the changing face of England, and it is part of
the historian's business to decipher that unwritten
record, "to construe"—in Maitland's phrase—"the
testimony of our fields and walls and hedges."

Although field-work is not the least important
part of his research, it will bear full fruit only when
conjoined with research among private muniments
and public archives. A vast and seemingly endless
range of documentary materials will claim attention,
beginning perhaps with an Anglo-Saxon charter of
the eighth century and ending with the files of the
local newspaper. Mastery of these records implies a
degree of palaeographical, diplomatic, and linguistic
skill not easily or quickly attained. The maturest
scholarship is not out of place in local history.

To feel equally at home in all the centuries is beyond most men's capacity. Nevertheless, the local historian should not allow himself to be too strongly repelled by any era with which he has to deal, for a lack of sympathetic insight can ruin even the most scholarly performance. If he sees the age of Anselm and Edmund Rich as a period of unmitigated squalor, or again if the age we live in fills him only with nostalgia for the good old days of Queen Victoria or Queen Anne or Queen Elizabeth I, he is unlikely to make the best of his theme.

In sketching the ideal attributes of our historian we have specified ripe scholarship, wide reading, wider sympathies, and sturdy legs. It is much to ask, but to these requirements let us add one more. The local historian should be no stranger to the art of composition. This is the more necessary because his subject has never been a favourite with the reading public. Yet the slow and often painful process by which a rural or urban community is brought into existence and nursed up to its full strength is not accomplished without tensions, often dramatic in their force and effect. The same may be said of the possibly more rapid and still more painful process of disintegration. The historian should possess a sufficiently vivid narrative gift to make those tensions felt. If local history has too often appeared dull, relying overmuch on the ready-made sympathy of the native or adopted inhabitant, it is because the writer has either misconceived his theme or lacked the imagination and literary skill required to communicate its interest. The perfect history of a town or village will be one that can be read with pleasure even by people who have never set foot in the place.

It will be obvious that local history as defined here

is anything but an elementary study. Indeed, since at its fullest range it lays most of the other historical disciplines under contribution, a good case could be made out for regarding it as the most advanced of them all. This doubtless is why it still has far to go in achieving academic and public recognition. For although it has called forth a whole library of books and enlisted the devotion of many fine scholars from Camden onwards, it remains in its infancy still. Its technique has not yet been perfected, and its *raison d'être* is far from being generally understood.

We cannot be sure that it would have fared much better if it had been monopolized from the first by professional scholars. In point of fact, the portion of the field which they have cultivated is tiny compared with the vast area that has yet to be explored. There is work in plenty waiting to be done by willing hands. This being so, it is fortunate that local history possesses a seemingly inexhaustible attraction for the amateur. For the veriest novice can help to collect materials, and enjoy himself in doing so. There are field-names to be rescued from oblivion, reminiscences of old inhabitants to be gathered and sifted, family papers to be scrutinized. These and a host of other tasks call for no technical equipment, or none that cannot be acquired with a little patience. A respect for historic truth and a capacity for accurate recording will carry the beginner a long way. Local history is not only a challenge to the most highly trained master of historical techniques; it is also—and long may it remain!—the last refuge of the non-specialist.[1]

[1] It now has its own admirable textbook: W. G. Hoskins, *Local History in England*, 1959.

LOCAL HISTORY
IN THE UNIVERSITY

An Inaugural Lecture
delivered in the University of Leicester
26 May 1964

By H. P. R. Finberg

IT is not given to many men to deliver two inaugural lectures in one and the same university;
but I have come uncomfortably close to that
experience. In 1952, when the University College
of Leicester did me the honour of placing me in
charge of its Department of English Local History,
I was invited to inaugurate my tenure of office by
delivering a public lecture, and I accepted the in-
vitation; but when the lecture came to be published,
I was told, gently but firmly, that it takes a professor
to deliver an inaugural; so we described it on the
title-page as an "introductory" lecture.[1] The truth
is that I was ill prepared by early training to appreciate the niceties of academic class-distinction. As a
small boy at a preparatory school I was initiated into
the art of swimming by a personage as bald as an
eggshell, and of approximately the same shape.
With or without academic warrant, he was styled
"the Professor." At rare intervals he would himself
descend into the water and regale us with a series of
aquatic feats more impressive as physical contor-
tions than as examples of professorial deportment.
He was my first professor. Years passed, and I went

[1] *The Local Historian and his Theme*, reprinted *supra*, pp. 1–24.

45

to the university; but the professors at Oxford in my time knew their business far too well to let me come within hailing distance. And so it was not until I came to Leicester many years later, with half a lifetime of non-academic work behind me, that I at last had an opportunity of discovering what professors really are. Even now I have not fully recovered from the impact of that revelation.

Today, however, by the generous decision of our governing bodies, for which I am indeed grateful, I find myself a member of that select company. It is now my duty and privilege not merely to practise and teach English Local History, but to profess it *ex cathedra*. When I have expressed, however inadequately, my thanks for such a signal honour, what more should I say? The custom on these occasions of paying a more or less glowing tribute to one's predecessor is one with which, at a pinch, I could no doubt comply; but it would come with an ill grace from me, since I am succeeding myself. On looking through my "introductory" discourse of 1952, I find little or nothing in it that I would wish to unsay now; and in a more recent publication I have developed the argument in fuller detail.[1] Nevertheless, although the subject has numbered fine scholars among its votaries from the sixteenth century onwards, there has never until now been a Professor of English Local History, and the Leicester department has attracted a good deal of public notice by the very fact of being unique. In such circumstances I should be failing in a due sense of the

[1] 'Local History', in H. P. R. Finberg (ed.), *Approaches to History*, Routledge and Kegan Paul, 1962, pp. 111–25, reprinted *supra*, pp. 25–44.

occasion if I did not attempt to lay before you some further thoughts on local history considered as an academic discipline.

There are other reasons for studying history besides the fact that it helps us to understand the world we live in; but it does help us to understand the world we live in, and if only on that account its future seems tolerably well assured, for all the growing emphasis on technology and the natural sciences. But if the proverbial visitor from another planet should take the trouble to examine the organization of historical studies in the universities and university colleges of Great Britain, he would note some puzzling features. Leaving aside the few remaining institutions in which a solitary Professor of History and his staff are apparently expected to cope with the entire human past, he would find that History as such is distinguished at Swansea and Southampton from something called Modern History, and at Brighton from European History. No fewer than ten institutions appear to believe that history can be divided into three categories: ancient, medieval, and modern, though I should add that the Ancient History studied at Edinburgh turns out on closer inspection to be Ancient Scottish History. Modern History is not recognized, at least under that name, at Bristol; Kent as yet has no use for any other; and Oxford, unlike Cambridge, has no chair of Medieval History.

There are other classifications which cut clean across the chronological scheme. One very large class confines itself to the history of some particular sphere of human activity. Here, as if to justify Napoleon's taunt that we are a nation of shopkeepers, Economic History leads the way, with seventeen professors and I know not how many other teachers. But the things of the spirit are not neglected: Ecclesiastical (or 'Church') History and the History of Art (or 'Fine Art') run it pretty close. University College London teaches the history of Political Thought, and Manchester—appropriately enough—that of Economic Thought. Peace has been neglected so far, but the History of War has its professor at Oxford. Farther afield we encounter such rarities as the solitary lecturers in Social History at Manchester and Business History at Glasgow.

I shall say nothing about Archaeology, because although it enjoys a large and flourishing establishment of its own in several universities, any claim it may have to be regarded as an independent study rests upon a concept which archaeologists themselves now repudiate as obsolete. It was plausible only so long as they were supposed to confine their researches to a past remote beyond the reach of written records, a past ending if not before Ancient History began, at any rate well before the dawn of Modern History. Today no one thinks of their function in those terms. We find them busy excavating the sites of English villages deserted in the fifteenth century, while others search out early monuments of the Industrial Revolution. But in thus immensely broadening its range, Archaeology has revealed itself more plainly as the ancillary discipline it really is: in other words, as a combination of highly specialized techniques, the true and ultimate function of which is to illuminate the subject-matter of History.

Even without Archaeology, the posts I have

enumerated form a large and motley establishment. But do they fall into any kind of rational
pattern, reflecting a clearly defined conception of
what history really is? The formal division of the
subject into three chronological categories, ancient,
medieval, and modern, dates from a time when
Greco-Roman antiquity was thought of as being
separated from our present civilization by a period
of Gothic barbarism, for which a seventeenth-century Dutch professor invented the term 'Middle
Ages'. It expresses an idea, or set of ideas, which
becomes less and less tenable as time goes on, and
when applied in any but a west-European context,
it looks even sillier than it does here at home. (I
might quote, for instance, a recent work entitled
The Mediaeval History of the Coast of Tanganyika.)
Again, what theoretical justification can be offered
for dividing human experience into separate com-
partments and attempting to write a history of each?
One of our honorary graduates, Sir John Summer-
son, reviewing a volume of the Oxford History of
Art the other day, felt constrained to ask what was
meant by art in this context, and to express a doubt
whether any satisfactory way could be found of writing its history.[1] Economic History, again, revolves
around a figment called Economic Man; that is to
say, it assumes that human beings engaged in winning a livelihood can be isolated, for purposes of
study, from the same human beings engaged in
painting pictures or studying in a university or
playing cricket or singing hymns in church, and
that it is intellectually profitable so to isolate them:
neither of which propositions is self-evidently true.

[1] *Antiquaries Journal*, XLIII, 1963, p. 322.

In hinting that they are debatable, however, I would not be understood to prejudge the outcome of the debate. Things which look odd on paper sometimes turn out quite well in practice. Not so long ago another honorary graduate of this university moved from the chair of Medieval History at Cambridge into that of Modern History without making any noticeable change of course in his research and writing. I doubt if the professor of Military History at Oxford attempts to talk or write about war in abstraction from the political and economic circumstances of the belligerents, and I know that economic historians often overstep, naturally and rightly, the ostensible limitations of their subject. A very great French historian has remarked that *homo religiosus, homo oeconomicus, homo politicus,* and similar abstractions, are convenient only so long as they are not allowed to cramp us; but he adds that if we concentrate our attention on these and suchlike fragments of human experience for their own sakes, not only shall we never know humanity in the round: we shall never really come to understand the fragments.[1]

The third category we must notice may be provisionally—but only provisionally—denominated territorial. It is represented by departments of English, Welsh, Scottish, French, Dutch, and American History, among others. And if there is to be division of labour among historians, as I think there obviously must, here at any rate we have a rational scheme of division. It is rational because our object should be not only to present the historian with a quantitatively manageable theme, but also to

[1] Marc Bloch, *Métier d'Historien,* 1952, pp. 76, 78.

give him an intelligible field of study. And these divisions do so. The history of England or of France is an intelligible field of study in a sense which cannot be so securely predicated either of modern history as such or of abstractions like art or science. It is so not because it deals with only a limited portion of the earth's surface, but because the human beings born and domiciled in England and France form, and have long formed, distinct communities, each with a life-story of its own.

For historical purposes I have elsewhere interpreted 'community' as meaning "a set of people occupying an area with defined territorial limits and so far united in thought and action as to feel a sense of belonging together, in contradistinction from the many outsiders who do not belong."[1] As far back as we can probe into the human past the earth has been peopled by groups answering to that description, groups of human beings and as such distinguished, says Aristotle, from hives of bees by their moral perceptions and the power of speech, with all that these imply. Now if we want to understand the species to which we belong, we must make a study of those communities, for—again I quote Aristotle—one must be either more or less than man, either a god or a wild beast, to live outside one. And since the future is unknowable, our study can only be of their past: in other words, a historical study.

Thus whatever may be true of the other themes which engage the attention of historians, the study of local, national, and supra-national communities as such is at least theoretically justified. And that being so, Leicester was taking a rational course,

[1] p. 33 *supra*.

though an unprecedented one, seventeen years ago, when it set up a Department of English Local History. For the theme of local history, as the department has constantly proclaimed, is the Origin, Growth, Decline, and Fall of the local community. By 'local' here we mean, of course, a rural or urban community smaller than the community of the realm and forming part of it, just as the community of the realm usually forms part of a larger, supranational entity. And in speaking of origin, growth, decline, and fall, we are defining the theme at its fullest extension; it is certainly not implied that we must wait until a given community is dead before attempting to write its history.

But, it may be said, granting that local history is or can be an intelligible field of study, are the qualities it develops in the student such as to justify us in giving it a place in the academic sun? I shall not attempt to answer this question categorically, for every one of my hearers will probably have his own idea of what can and should be expected from a university education. Instead, if you will bear with me, I will speak briefly of some personal experiences which may suggest part of the answer.

When first I took up active work in local history, I found, as local historians in England very often do find, that the earliest document relating to the community which interested me was a royal charter, one of those which have come down to us, in number between two and three thousand, from before the Norman Conquest. It is a grave reproach to English scholarship that we have no satisfactory edition of the whole corpus. Most of the charters were collected and printed without annotation by J. M.

Kemble more than a century ago. In 1885 Walter de Gray Birch began to publish an edition with better texts, but he did not carry it beyond the reign of Edgar, so that we still have to fall back on Kemble for charters issued between 975 and 1066. The charter I had before me was dated 981, so it was not in Birch; and Kemble, applying the only form oj criticism he allowed himself, had marked it with an asterisk, signifying that he doubted its authenticity. This put me in a quandary, for one cannot build a sound historical edifice on the basis of a spurious charter. Now if any question arose concerning the charter which Her present Majesty granted to this university in 1957, proofs of its genuineness could be adduced without much difficulty, in number and strength sufficient to satisfy a court of law. I know now that for a charter of King Ethelred II this cannot be done; the most that criticism can do is to answer more or less cogently such objections as may be urged against it. But at that time, isolated as I was by professional duties of another kind from any contact with the world of scholarship, I supposed that in some corner of that world an expert would be found who could declare oracularly whether the charter of 981 was genuine or not. So I wrote to a historian whom I had not met since we were fellow-members of an undergraduate club some twenty years before, and I asked him to put me on the track of such an expert. He is a very well-known, distinguished scholar, and I am glad to say that we have since happily renewed our youthful acquaintance, all the more gratefully on my side because he conferred upon me the inestimable boon of never answering my letter. His silence put me in the position of a workman who is obliged to construct his own tools. Now the criticism of Anglo-Saxon charters not only demands a competent knowledge of two languages, or rather of three languages: Old English, Latin, and bad Latin; it is also, or should be, an exercise combining the techniques of history, topography, diplomatics, palaeography, and textual emendation. Far be it from me to claim anything approaching mastery of even one of these; but I did manage to grasp enough of the rudiments to produce a new edition of King Ethelred's charter, and in so doing to dispel the aura of suspicion cast over it by Kemble's asterisk.

At a later stage in my researches I had occasion to go through a series of episcopal registers. In one of them I found the text of a decree by which a thirteenth-century bishop deposed the abbot of the most important monastery in the diocese, and gave his reasons for this drastic move. He charged the abbot with scandalous maladministration. There was nothing improbable in the charge; not all abbots were or are good managers. But a little later I learnt from an entry in the Calendar of Close Rolls that some months before his deposition the abbot had begun an action at law against the bishop's steward. Later still I found in the Calendar of Miscellaneous Inquisitions the report of a special enquiry conducted by a royal commissioner, in the course of which three separate juries testified that the bishop's steward had been plundering the abbey right and left. Finally, in an unprinted Assize Roll at the Public Record Office I found yet another jury showing unmistakably that their sympathies lay wholly with the abbot. Here was an interesting object-lesson in the handling of documentary evidence, a vivid reminder that a document may be unimpeachably genuine, like the bishop's register, and yet not tell the truth, or not the whole truth: that, in short, authenticity must be sharply distinguished from veracity.

Some time before reaching that point, I had hunted up the eighteenth-century estate maps and copied the old name of every field on to the modern six-inch Ordnance maps. The area of approximately eighteen square miles with which I had to deal contained old houses of great architectural merit, as well as the ruined abbey and a fine parish church, a canal the construction of which represented a notable engineering feat in its day, the grass-grown quays of a deserted little river-port, an imposing railway viaduct, and extensive remains of copper-mines now worked out but in their time the richest in the world. All this in a setting of the utmost natural beauty. It was therefore a pleasure as well as a duty to explore nearly every acre on foot. To walk over a field called Forges at the farthest limit of a manor the lord of which at one time wielded powers of life and death, and to know from the name that here stood his 'forches', *furcae*, or gallows; to trace the line of a dried-up watercourse along the steep side of a wooded valley, to find that it led up to and straight through a huge pile called Raven's Rock, to crawl into the opening and to find evidence in the shape of interior chisel-marks that it had been made before gunpowder came into use for blasting, and to identify the watercourse from a contemporary manuscript as one made at the behest of King Edward IV to provide power for the argentiferous

E

lead-mines in the neighbouring parish; to find amid lush meadows the crumbling walls of a deserted farmstead where, according to local tradition, Sir Francis Drake, when he had made his fortune, would have liked to settle down, and to notice lying among the nettles a piece of worked stone, all that remained perhaps of the little private chapel standing in 1388, when the owner, head of a yeoman family domiciled on that spot from time immemorial, obtained licence to have mass celebrated there: these and other such experiences, agreeable in themselves, were also highly stimulating to the historical imagination.

If I have indulged perhaps overlong in these personal reminiscences, it is because I think they help to answer our question concerning the educational value of local history. A pursuit in which the laborious accumulation of data and accurate transcription of documents are merely the first steps; which obliges one to sift evidence, checking one document against another; which keeps the imagination as well as the intellect at work; which more perhaps than any other form of historical enquiry quickens the sense of place and enables one to visualize the background against which a rural or urban community acted out the drama of its communal existence; and which imposes the final obligation of constructing a narrative precise and vivid enough to re-create that community in the fullness of its life and vigour: this is surely not a trivial pursuit, but one of which the intellectual and imaginative content render it not unworthy of a place beside the other arts and sciences cultivated in a university.

A place, then, in the university; but what place?

It might seem that this question was answered once for all at Leicester in 1947, when the then University College decided to set up an autonomous department with a mandate covering the history of local communities all over England. But in the life of a twentieth-century university seventeen years is a long time. Faces change; old trains of thought are forgotten; and new claims arise. Moreover, I can imagine a specious but misleading analogy being drawn between historical and natural science. Two years ago our Professor of Biochemistry, in his inaugural lecture, gave reasons for holding that the best interests of the biological sciences and of the university as a whole would be served by grouping those sciences into a single academic unit, a school housing under one roof a number of specialities and perhaps containing "several chairs uncommitted by title." Whether his colleagues in the Faculty of Science interpreted this, in the language of the Stock Exchange, as a proposal for amalgamation by exchange of shares or as a 'take-over bid', it was at any rate supported by weighty arguments both practical and theoretical; and to these last I shall return in a moment, since it is here that a misleading parallel might be drawn.

After all—some one may say—whatever the differences between local, national, and ecumenical history, they have one great thing in common. They all deal with the human past; they are all, in a word, History. Their techniques of analysis and synthesis are fundamentally the same; the same rules of evidence hold good for all three; the documents on which they rely are not different in kind. Why then put them into separate departments? Why not combine them in one great School of History, with "several chairs uncommitted by title," or, as one might put it, professors professing nothing in particular?

The argument, I submit, will hardly convince any one who looks below the surface. Professor Kornberg told us that "in all branches of experimental biology, the barriers which separate one biologist from another are tending to disappear," and a unitary approach is being imposed on all concerned by the very success of their investigations. "It does not require expert knowledge," he said, "to perceive that a lion and a dandelion differ from each other and from a bacterium, but these obvious differences which strike the eye have tended to obscure the fact that many basic features are common to all forms of life. One of the main achievements of biochemistry has been to reveal these basic features and to indicate that variations amongst living things are but variations on common themes, accentuated by the processes of evolution over aeons of time."[1] The biochemist, then, seeks out and identifies, at the starting-point of lengthy evolutionary processes, a unitary principle of Life, and makes that the object of his study. By contrast, the historian is concerned not with unity but with diversity. He takes for granted that historic processes revolve around a being called Man, and he sets himself to re-enact the life of human aggregates as lived in all their rich variety through the centuries. If every man were just like his neighbours, there would be no employment for the biographer; and it is because

[1] H. L. Kornberg, *The Unity of Life*, Leicester University Press, 1962, pp. 19, 21.

nations differ that each of them has a history of its own.

And not only nations: the same is true of communities both larger and smaller than the nation. In the local, the national, and the supra-national community we have three distinct manifestations of social life, with different extensions in space and time: in other words, three distinct fields of study for the historian.

I will not now repeat or elaborate the arguments I have used elsewhere to demonstrate that the nation is not the same thing as the village or the town writ large. Instead let me quote a single illustration of the difference between them. In 1574 the grammar school of Leicester was remodelled by the locally all-powerful earl of Huntingdon in strict accordance with the most advanced principles of the Elizabethan religious settlement. At that very time, and throughout the reign, the grammar school of Burnley, under far different influences, was sending forth one recruit after another to the seminaries in Flanders where the recusant clergy were trained for the English Catholic mission. In the broad perspectives of national history such contrasts tend to disappear. We know that the earl of Huntingdon was on the winning side and took Leicester with him; we know too that the victory was not quite total; but the national historian can scarcely be blamed for passing lightly over such details as the obstinate conservatism of Burnley.[1] The local his-

[1] "The historian will not in ordinary circumstances need to take cognizance of a single discontented peasant or discontented village. But millions of discontented peasants in thousands of villages are a factor which no historian will ignore."—E. H. Carr, *What is*

torian, on the other hand, when he observes one Elizabethan market town being carried along with the national tide, and another battling not altogether ineffectually against it, is made vividly aware that the local community has not always conformed promptly and gracefully to patterns of thought and conduct imposed upon it from above.

Local, national, and ecumenical history, then, deal with three interrelated but yet distinct forms of social life, each with its own chronology and its own spatial extension. And once that is understood, it is logical, in a twentieth-century university where research and teaching are organized in professorial departments according to subject-matter, for Local History to be established in an autonomous department of its own. Any other status would imply a failure to recognize the true nature of the subject. It was largely this lack of understanding which caused Reading, after setting up the first academic post in local history, to discontinue it four years later, thereby throwing away the position of leadership it might have taken in this field, and leaving the initiative open to be seized by Leicester thirty-five years later.[1] The setting up of our department

History?, Macmillan, 1961, p. 44. For "historian" here read "national historian."

[1] In 1912 the Research Fellow in Local History at Reading was appointed Professor of Modern History, and the fellowship was allowed to lapse. The terms in which the Principal of the University College, W. M. Childs, referred to "the study of local history as a means of illustrating the wider study of national history" show that the history of the local community was not yet held to be a subject worth pursuing for its own sake.—Prefatory Note to F. M. Stenton's *Early History of the Abbey of Abingdon*, Reading, 1913, p. iv.

in 1947, with a mandate covering the history of urban and rural communities all over England and not only in Leicestershire or the east midlands, has been hailed in other universities, and by a very large extramural public, as local history's Declaration of Independence, proof that after a period of trial and error prolonged over four centuries and more than one false start, the subject has come of age, and its exponents are not to be regarded as mere antiquarian triflers, or drudges with no other function than that of providing footnotes for somebody else's History of England.

Now there are people who, when they have to sign a hotel register, will describe themselves as British rather than as English or Scots; and a day may come when they will think and speak of themselves as members of some even larger community. Such things have been known before. The third-century Briton proud to denominate himself a citizen of Rome; in the sixteenth century a Thomas More taking his stand upon an ecumenical tradition above and beyond the competence of any local king or parliament; a twentieth-century Marxist who might find himself in a dilemma if the interests of his country should clash with those of international communism: all these in their different ways personify the larger loyalties. It is therefore not extravagant to speak of a possible future in which patriotism as at present understood will be no more dynamic a motive than the mild sentimental attachment some people still cherish for their native village. But if that time should come, what will the student know of the genus Man and of the species Englishman unless history re-creates for him the background against which the national poet wrote of "this sceptered isle . . . this precious stone set in the silver sea"? The thoughts and feelings which inspired those lines, and which nerved men to action on occasions of great peril such as the Spanish Armada or the Battle of Britain, are facts as real as any phenomenon studied by the chemist in his laboratory, and if ever they should recede into the past, it will be the historian's plain duty to bring them back to life in the consciousness of his disciples.

We are still near enough to the national state at the zenith of its power to recapture without difficulty a sense of its historical importance. It is not so easy to project our vision into the minds of local patriots for whom their own town or village was the centre of the universe. At a time when metropolitan boroughs with famous names are allowing themselves to be snuffed out of existence with only faint murmurs of protest, it needs an effort on our part to conjure up remembrance of the city of Exeter refusing to admit the Norman conqueror within its walls except upon its own terms; or the county of Kent appearing by its spokesmen before the justices in eyre in 1313 and demanding that when their inherited customs diverged from the common law the custom of Kent should prevail; or the inhabitants of the Isle of Axholme in 1650, answering Parliament's demand for compliance with measures destructive of their traditional husbandry by calling it "a Parliament of clouts" and declaring roundly that "they could make as good a Parliament themselves." For most of us, in short, the local community is already as much a thing of the past as I have pictured the national community becoming some generations hence. And here too a large tract of social experience is involved. It is the business of the local historian to put that experience on record, and we should encourage him to do so, for unless he does, our knowledge and understanding of human relationships will be sadly impoverished.

At a time like the present, when the power and importance of the national state are visibly on the wane, it is not surprising to hear voices urging a change of direction in historical studies; and those voices may well grow more insistent as time goes on. Having said that the future is unknowable, I shall only invite ridicule if I indulge in prophecy; but it does seem not unlikely that the next generation of students will be hearing more about Russia, China, and America than about "1066 and all that," or, shall we say, more about western Europe as a whole than about the Wars of the Roses and the precise shades of difference between one group of Whig partisans and another. If so, if the fortunes of the national state cease to occupy the central position they have occupied in our historical studies until recently, the present widespread interest in local history is likely to be intensified rather than diminished. In my introductory discourse twelve years ago I may have seemed to imply that people are moved to take up local history chiefly by nostalgia for a vanished and supposedly more agreeable past. Of some this may be true; but I think the real secret of attraction is the relatively small scale of the subject. The horizons opened up by ecumenical history are dazzling in their immensity. People turn from them with relief and quickened interest to something nearer home, nearer even than Whitehall. It is the local historian's great advantage that he can explore his chosen area on foot and talk to its inhabitants. But the immediacy of his theme is more than merely topographical. The hamlet, village, or town is, next to the family, the smallest social unit we can study, and no other brings us into such intimate touch with past generations of living, breathing fellow-countrymen.

Whether or not this is the secret of attraction, it is an unquestionable fact that a very large and heterogeneous public now takes an enthusiastic interest in local history. From this widespread popular interest the subject draws much of its vitality. The circumstance also invests our department, as the only existing university Department of English Local History, with responsibilities not limited by academic frontiers. And now that the department speaks with professorial authority, it is incumbent on me to declare how we interpret those responsibilities.

Our first duty, as I see it, is to propagate a reasoned conception of the subject. Local history still suffers from a lack of theoretical discussion. It will take more than one academic lifetime to undo the mistakes of the pioneers. Popular interest and zeal are not enough: they need to be reinforced and guided by a proper understanding of the local historian's business. Far too many people still find themselves in the position of the amateur who wrote to me some weeks ago to ask for guidance. He explained that for five years he had been accumulating notes on the history of a Wiltshire village, but he was quite at a loss to interpret his materials or put them into shape; and he concluded by saying, with cheerful pessimism, that his collection now lacked only the detailed genealogies of the lords of the manor to make it quite ready for the dust-bin. Such appeals impose on us a duty of missionary effort. We have to work out and persistently expound a theory of local history that will provide a sound basis for the work of its practitioners both inside and outside the university.

A student of mathematics would not get very far unless he knew his multiplication table, and one cannot master a foreign language until one has learnt to conjugate its verbs. Just so, in history, there is an aggregate of elementary fact which must be assimilated before the subject can be pursued at all fruitfully. It was doubtless not much fun for Sir Thomas Bertram's daughters to learn by heart "the chronological order of the kings of England, with the dates of their accession, and most of the principal events of their reigns . . . Yes, and of the Roman emperors as low as Severus," but besides giving them something to plume themselves upon by contrast with their cousin Fanny, it did provide a framework into which more advanced knowledge could have been securely fitted had their studies been prolonged. It is the business of the schools to equip their pupils with this apparatus of elementary fact, and not to send them forth as sketchily informed as that elderly Yorkshireman who after listening for an hour and a half to a lecture on the dissolution of the monasteries given by an experienced extramural tutor, rose at question-time and said: "Do you mean us to understand that those old monks were all Roman Catholics?"

I am told that the method of study by what are

called 'projects' is gaining ground in the schools. The pupil is given a theme and turned loose to gather such relevant information as he can find out for himself. Having never taught schoolchildren myself, I am not competent to pronounce an opinion on the merits of this plan, but I imagine that it does help to arouse and activate the pupil's interest. I imagine, too, that the materials need to be fairly close at hand. Elementary textbooks will supply regnal names and dates, but the local scene will supply monuments which the pupil can sketch or photograph, and other visible evidence in plenty. Hence the growing popularity of local history in schools. Many schools now organize lectures, excursions, field-clubs, and exhibitions, in all of which local history plays a part. The secondary modern school, being less dominated than the grammar school by the need to prepare its pupils for public examinations, gives particular attention to this local approach.

On the other hand, in any future that can be foreseen the examinations which no schoolchild altogether escapes will not be examinations in local history. Hence the function of local history in school is, and is likely to remain, ancillary. This was indeed the place assigned to it in the earliest state paper which accorded it a place in the national system of education. A circular from the Board of Education in 1908 required teachers to make "constant reference to the history of the locality *as illustrative of the general history*."[1] In other words, the pupil is not to concern himself with the story of the local community as such. He is still learning his "1066 and

[1] Board of Education Circular 599, dated 25 November 1908.

all that," and local illustrations are brought in merely to lighten the tedium for him.

Later he goes to a university and tries for an honours degree in history. At first he will be fully occupied in extending his range of factual knowledge, filling in the gaps in what he learnt at school. But even the amount of specialization implied in an honours course is expected to be truly educational, to turn out educated men and women, not just walking encyclopaedias. Therefore, since knowledge of facts develops only the memory, knowledge alone will not suffice: we expect an educated man to have acquired the skills necessary for organizing his knowledge and interpreting the facts. At this stage, accordingly, the student moves on from the textbooks to the original sources. He is encouraged to think for himself, and required to put his thoughts in writing; and to make this possible, he concentrates on a chosen 'special subject'.

It is at this point that I believe the Department of English Local History can usefully co-operate with the Departments of History and of Economic History. For local history is not a body of knowledge which can be imparted through the medium of textbooks. And even if it were, it is not the knowledge of which an undergraduate student has most need. I say this because the local community is the least crudely powerful of social entities. However vigorous its life and ethos, however stubborn its resistance to external pressures, it cannot escape them altogether. Hence the history of Europe and of England will do more to enlighten us about the history of Leicester or Barchester than *vice versa*. The knowledge of national and international history which the undergraduate has been acquiring are indispensable to the local historian. It is at that point in his course where the acquisition of knowledge begins to be coupled with the development of historical skill, that local history, in the form of carefully designed 'special subjects', can help the undergraduate by introducing him to original sources and pointing the way to their interpretation. To begin earlier would be to build on sand.

Suppose now that our student, having taken his degree, wishes to engage in post-graduate work. He has learnt his "1066 and all that"; he has had some practice in weighing historical evidence, and acquired some insight into the nature of historical processes. Now, when he is ready to undertake original research, local history may legitimately exert its full attraction. He will have to do a lot of fact-finding about his chosen town or village, but all the political, ecclesiastical, and economic history that he has learnt will be pressed into service when he sets himself to interpret the facts and organize his narrative. Since the greater part of English local history has yet to be written, there is ample room for all the skills of which a historian is capable.

The Robbins committee looks forward to a considerable expansion of post-graduate studies in the near future, and remarks that since it is plainly impossible for all universities to excel in all subjects, advanced work of high quality will inevitably be concentrated in institutions known to offer unique facilities in certain fields.[1] So far as local history is

---

[1] *Higher Education* (Report of the Committee appointed by the Prime Minister under the Chairmanship of Lord Robbins), 1963, p. 106.

concerned, Leicester is already in that position. Since our university acquired the power to grant its own degrees, the Department of English Local History has ceased to be one in which the chief, if not the only, duty of its members was held to be the prosecution and publication of their own research-work. In other words, it has ceased to be a research department pure and simple, and is now more properly described as a graduate school, with rami-fications extending, as I have tried to show, on one side into the field of undergraduate studies, and on the other into that of extramural education. In all these spheres it is our duty to uphold the status of the subject as a branch of scholarship. Any idea that local history is a comparatively soft option must be firmly dispelled. We have to show by teaching and —so far as in us lies—by the example of our own work that it is as rigorous and exacting a study as any other academic discipline. Its perspectives are admittedly not so wide as those of national and international history, but then our curiosity extends to every corner of the local scene. Others may specialize in this period or that, in ecclesiastical or parliamentary or economic history: the local his-torian, for whom the urban or rural community is one entire whole, must embrace them all.

I should have liked to deal with a possible criticism that local history as understood at Leices-ter, so far from being a trivial pursuit, makes de-mands too far-reaching to be met successfully by any but a dedicated few. I might also have discussed the place of team-work in our study, and touched upon the possibility that twentieth-century tech-niques of communication may presently diminish the importance of books and articles in the dissemination of our work. But time presses, and I forbear. I hope I have said enough to set the ball of discussion rolling—outside the university if not within it. If so, it only remains for me to thank the University of Leicester, in the name of local historians everywhere, for all it has done to protect and foster our subject.

HOW NOT TO WRITE
LOCAL HISTORY

By H. P. R. Finberg

A N Y one who wishes to avoid writing local history will find it perfectly easy to do so : he has only to switch on the radio or television; or he can just go to sleep. For present purposes, however, let us assume that somebody, somewhere, wants an occupation of a quasi-intellectual nature, and feeling no call to engage in some generally respected and lucrative pursuit, is determined at all costs to write the history of a local community. It is for his sake that I write; I shall try to show him how to reach the standard of performance that is expected of him: in other words, how to achieve that monumental flatness, tedium, and lack of acceptance which has been the hallmark of local history as too commonly practised.

It may be objected: "What need is there of teaching on this subject? The shelves of every big library creak under a dead weight of books, almost every one of which is a model of the way not to write local history. With so many exemplars to guide him, how can the beginner possibly go wrong?"

There is force in this contention. On the other hand, it is possible that our student might waste a certain amount of time hesitating over the choice of models. Moreover, while native genius may have saved the authors of those books from the need of taking thought, mere ordinary talent must be improved by study and practice. For these reasons it may be useful to set forth one or two general precepts, making explicit the principles which have guided the hands of the masters in this dim field of study. I ought perhaps to add, in the spirit of the novelist who declares that every character in this story is fictitious, that when I speak with less than entire respect of our predecessors, I am referring mainly to local historians who are already dead, though I may inadvertently include one or two who still move and breathe and are unaware how dead they are.

The first rule to be laid down is one that admits of no exception. Since fortunes are not made by writing local history, the writer's impulse can only proceed from a genuine enthusiasm for the subject, and the rule is: TO ASSUME AN EQUAL ENTHUSIASM IN THE READER. In his single-minded devotion to the *genius loci*, the historian finds an endless fascination in every aspect of his chosen theme, and he takes it for granted that his readers will approach it in the same spirit; or rather, in his modesty, he assumes that nobody will read his narrative unless he cares about the place at least as much as the writer does. This assumption is usually correct; and it has the further merit of being immensely laboursaving. A historian who feels himself under an obligation to woo the interest of as many readers as possible, including people who have never set foot in the parish, will have to take thought about his narrative; and, as we all know, there is no pain like the pain of thought. He will have to introduce some order, art, and method into the work, to exercise a modicum of selection and compression, to polish up

his literary style. But the golden rule I have enunciated will save him all this trouble. No need to shape
his narrative, to give it a beginning, a middle, and
an end; no need to enliven it with graphic touches,
to season it from time to time with the salt of irony,
to work on the imagination and sympathies of the
audience. He can go straight ahead, spilling the contents of his notebooks pell-mell over the page, never
pausing to ask himself whether he is becoming a
bore. Addressing himself only to an imaginary company of like-minded enthusiasts, he goes on adding
yet another to the long list of local histories which
only the most pressing curiosity will impel anyone
to read.

Now since our historian is by definition an en-
thusiast, and since he obviously depends on some
other source for his livelihood, he will have scant
leisure for comparative study. Even if he has any
curiosity to spare for other parishes and other counties, it never occurs to him that some places are more
significant historically than others, and that his own
village may not need to be portrayed at the same
length as an ancient market town or a big manufacturing city. Thus the element of comparison is lacking; he never knows what is peculiar to his own
parish and what is common form. He finds that the
churchwardens from time to time spent money on
the destruction of vermin; that vagrants were driven
out of the parish with all convenient speed; and that
under the later Stuarts the parson was obliged to
certify that deceased parishioners were buried in
woollen shrouds. Happily unaware that the same
things were being done in parishes all over the
country, he naturally communicates these exciting

discoveries to the reader, who, let us hope, will be equally uninformed.

Odd creature as he is, the local historian is sufficiently human to have his likes and dislikes; in fact, he is often a crotchety character. And since he cannot hope to erupt into print very often, he treats the history of his town or village as a heaven-sent opportunity for airing his crotchets. Every now and then he peppers its pages with fiery little outbursts against Henry VIII or Oliver Cromwell or the pope. This certainly gives the book a semblance of animation, but unfortunately it is not of a kind that really exhilarates the reader. He also has his antiquarian preferences: a passion for Gothic architecture, perhaps, which leads him to describe the church at unconscionable length, while never sparing a glance for the Georgian manor-house or some uniquely interesting farmstead.

An even more fruitful source of tedium is the landed gentry. Many a so-called history seems to have been constructed on the principle that nobody ever lived in the parish but the squire and his relations. Dr Joan Wake, that doughty champion of local studies at their best, remembers overhearing a conversation between two elderly gentlewomen in Northamptonshire. The village of Isham happened to be mentioned; whereupon one lady asked: "Who's living at Isham now?" To which her friend replied: "You know quite well that *nobody* has *ever* lived at Isham." An overpowering interest in the class to which the historians themselves belonged, or would have liked to belong, has cast a genealogical blight over English local history from which it is only now beginning to recover.

Then a feeling for romance, impelling the writer to fill his pages with picturesque or sentimental anecdotes, can do wonders in putting the reader off. The ghost of the white lady who flits about the manor-house; the underground passage alleged to lead from the priory to a nunnery some five miles off; the bed that Elizabeth I or Charles II may have slept in; the local skirmish between Cavaliers and Roundheads; the minor cases of bad language, assault, and bloodshed recorded in the manor court rolls: if enough space is given up to trivialities like these, the writer can be sure of leaving out the topics of most interest to an intelligent reader. In the history of a Cheshire village published a few years ago we read of a secret tunnel and a murdered nun. "She was murdered," says the writer, "because she broke her vows and married." We naturally wonder who did the deed, her husband or the abbess; but on this point curiosity remains unsatisfied. "It is not known what the date of the tragedy could be," he tells us candidly, "but her habit was black."

Most historians naturally feel more at home in one period than another. Two excellent local histories, Robo's *Medieval Farnham* and Fowler's *Medieval Sherborne*, make no pretence of carrying the story down into a period with which the authors felt unable to deal sympathetically. Contrast this with two other works, both of great merit in their different ways: Hine's *History of Hitchin*, and the more recent *History of Birmingham* by Gill and Briggs. Here the first thousand years or more are disposed of in about fifty pages, after which the writers settle down to write in earnest about the last century or two, which is all they really care about.

A FORESHORTENING OF HISTORICAL PERSPEC-
TIVE is one of the most common failings. It besets
national as well as local history, notably in the
Oxford History of England, which sets out to
cover some nineteen hundred and fifty years in
fifteen volumes, and devotes eight volumes to the
last four centuries. The truly great local historian,
when he appears, will deal faithfully with all
periods.

Not so the chronicler for whom I am prescrib-
ing. He will probably begin by quoting the Domesday reference to the place; or perhaps he will first
describe a round barrow and an earthwork which he
incorrectly declares to be a Roman camp. Then the
Domesday passage; and there is no better way of
unnerving the average reader at the outset than to
hurl a chunk of Domesday at him, without any
explanation of its terminology or so much as a hint
that scholars are not altogether certain what some
of the entries mean. Next, perhaps, a page about the
church, and one on the descent of the manor; after
which, having scampered through the first thousand years or so in fewer than a dozen pages, the
writer settles down to regale the public with his
gleanings from the parish registers, family papers,
and the local newspaper, interspersed with anecdotes about the local worthies and unworthies, and
finishing perhaps with a detailed account of the
festivities got up to celebrate a royal jubilee.

This distortion of the time-scheme is usually de-
fended on the ground that it is natural for a historian to write more fully when his materials become
more abundant. Natural, indeed, it may be; but
history is not a natural pursuit: it is a science and an

art. The mere accident that records have survived in plenty does not by itself invest a subject with historical significance. Of all the reasons which may impel a man to undertake a piece of historical research, the fact that documents bearing on the subject are abundant and accessible ought to weigh least. In reality, people who advance this plea only do so because their conception of historical evidence is an unduly narrow one. They are thinking too much about written and printed documents, not enough about farm names and field names and parish boundaries; not enough about the shapes and sizes of fields, the roads, the hedges, the visible pattern of settlement and cultivation. There is plenty of material for reconstructing the early history of a local community if only they would go out of doors and look for it. And seeing that the earlier centuries were in fact the formative period in the life of most local communities, there is no excuse for shirking this essential part of the historian's task.

Even when documents are plentiful, however, a really accomplished bungler will contrive to overlook them. The Reverend Roderick Dew comes to mind here as a conspicuous example. In his *History of the Parish and Church of Kilkhampton*, in Cornwall, he lamented that "the early churchwardens' accounts have not been preserved, and many ancient writings dealing with the church and church property have disappeared." Mr Dew was rector of Kilkhampton from 1908 to 1940. In 1948 his successor found in the vestry a rusty key which fitted the lock of an iron safe standing in the south-west corner of the church. The safe had been there, visible to all, as far back as the church cleaner could remember, and she was getting on for ninety. It proved to be crammed with parochial documents, including a fine set of churchwardens' accounts. It may be added that if Mr Dew had looked into Dugdale's *Monasticon*, that rich quarry for historians, he could have found a valuable clue to the history of Kilkhampton in the Saxon period. On the same page Joseph Fowler would have found—in fact, he did find—an equally valuable clue to the early history of Sherborne. He found it, and made nothing of it; so appreciation of his book must be qualified by the criticism that although he devotes a chapter to the pre-Saxon history of the place, he has missed a vital link in the evidence. It must be added that his ample quarto, which is full of topographical detail, includes no map, so that for readers who do not enjoy the privilege of living in Sherborne, many pages are completely unintelligible.

This brings us to another sovereign rule for the type of local historian we have in view. DON'T PROVIDE A MAP; or if you do, see that it is not drawn by a professional cartographer. Draw it yourself, or get it drawn by a friend who likes drawing maps. No matter that your or his idea of lettering would disgrace a class of infants. Make sure that several of the places named most frequently in the text are omitted from the map. Then let the blockmaker reduce it so drastically that most of the names become illegible; and finally let the binder insert it into the book in such a way that it tears every time you open it.

Many a local historian, sooner than face the exertion of shaping his facts into an ordered narrative, contents himself with printing the documents and leaving them to speak for themselves. Instead of a local history he produces a collection of raw materials. Even this admits of judicious mishandling. If you provide a transcript or translation which may justly be suspected of inaccuracy; if you leave out bits which you think unimportant, without giving any indication that you have done so; if you omit to state whether you are reproducing the original document or someone else's edition of it: then, in addition to presenting the materials in an undigested form, you will have done your best to rob them of any value to the trained student and the professional historian.

Some compilers pay homage to the muse of history after their fashion by serving up the contents of their notebooks in a kind of substitute for narrative. Each fact is presented in a paragraph quite unconnected with the paragraphs before and after, or connected only by some transparent thread like that phrase which came so readily to the pens of the young women who used to write the chapters on monastic life in the Victoria County Histories. Finding in the bishop's register two complaints against a monastery, with perhaps the better part of a century between them, the author gives the substance of the first denunciation, then opens a new paragraph saying: "*Things were no better* eighty-five years later." It need hardly be said that such a thin coating of narrative, far from making the mixture really palatable, only helps to set the reader's teeth on edge.

A word must be said, too, about the erudite person who thinks it unnecessary—if he thinks at all—

to render the jargon of bygone centuries into plain English. His pages are sprinkled with final concords, assizes of novel disseisin, inquisitions post mortem, fines and recoveries, writs of *Monstraverunt*, and the like. Here is another rule, then, complementary to the rule enunciated at the beginning of this discourse. ASSUME THAT THE READER IS ON A PAR WITH YOURSELF, not only in enthusiasm for the subject, but also IN ACQUAINTANCE WITH THE TECHNICALITIES. He ought to feel pleased and flattered; unfortunately, so perverse is human nature, he very seldom does.

The rule which bids us omit no triviality has for its corollary and counterpart that other rule bidding us EXCLUDE ALL THAT MATTERS. Faithful to this principle, the bungler is as maladroit in his silences as in anything he actually says. He gives the reader to understand that in what he calls the middle ages the village soil was cultivated under the open-field system; but where the fields were, whether there were two or three or more, what crops were grown, what stock was kept: on these topics he has not a word to say, and the suspicion arises that what he does say about the open fields is merely repeated from the textbooks. He mentions, without a flicker of curiosity, that "in some ancient records the place is styled a borough," but leaves you guessing how or when it acquired that status, whether it was co-extensive with the manor, and how it was governed. Changes of incumbent, he remarks, were unusually frequent in the sixteenth century, but he omits to say which parson, if any, was evicted as being too fervent a papist, and which because he was too extreme a protestant. He states that the common fields and pastures were enclosed in 1786, but whether this left the mass of inhabitants richer or poorer, and whether the population went up or down in consequence, remains obscure. The local industries come and go without a word of explanation. The history of a Lincolnshire parish, recently published, gives not the slightest hint that land may have been gained in past centuries by reclamation from the sea, or lost by coastal erosion, though the author has seen erosion taking place in his own lifetime.

A word or two now on the subject of references. The obvious and simple course of not giving any has much to commend it, to the publisher if to no one else, for footnotes are so expensive that he groans every time he sees one, and feels more keenly than ever that he has taken the book on against his better judgement. The reader, on the other hand, likes to have some clue to the evidence on which the work is built, and the author for his part is not as a rule unwilling to furnish it, for although references put him to a certain amount of trouble, they also provide the best possible opportunity for displaying his erudition. Here again the problem resolves itself into that of seeming to provide what is wanted but not really doing so. Even in the works of reputable historians examples of this technique are to be found. I once wasted the best part of a day in a vain attempt to follow up a footnote reference in Round's *Feudal England*. It consisted of the single word "Hermannus." The catalogue of the London Library gives twenty-one different authors named Hermann or Hermannus; and by the time I had looked up their dates in various works of reference, eliminated those who were not early enough, and ransacked the works of the remainder, darkness was beginning to fall. It was only some weeks later, through the kind help of a correspondent, that I discovered how the footnote ought to have been worded: it should have read "Migne, *Patrologia Latina*, CLVI, col. 983."

On another occasion, while reading H. S. Bennett's *Life on the English Manor*, I was forcibly struck by the statement that monastic landlords from time to time "caused their serfs"—to do what?—"to marry free women with inheritances." Feeling naturally curious to know more in detail how the abbots contrived to practise this refined form of cruelty, I endeavoured to follow up the author's footnote, which consisted of the one word "Walsingham." This presumably meant the St Albans chronicler Thomas Walsingham, but the eight volumes of his works printed in the Rolls Series threw no light on the subject; so I wrote to Mr Bennett for more information. He replied that while our country was at war he was not in a position to consult his notes. Thereupon I appealed to Dr Coulton, editor of the series in which Mr Bennett's work appeared, and a redoubtable stickler for accuracy. Thanks to his good offices, it was presently established that reference should have been made, not to Walsingham, but to *Rotuli Parliamentorum*, III, p. 319. And when I looked it up, it did not tell me how, if I had a serf, I should set about "causing" him to marry an heiress; it only said that when such marriages took place, as occasionally happened, they slipped through a loophole in the Statute of Mortmain.

Apart from the obvious course of giving no references at all, or giving the wrong ones, there are other ways in which they can be used to baffle the reader. One of them is the simple trick of quoting "Smith, *op. cit.*," thus forcing him to search through the undergrowth of perhaps a hundred and fifty pages before he can tell which of Smith's works is being cited. A more subtle device is to use printed sources, like the *Calendars of Close Rolls* and *Charter Rolls*, but to cite them in such a form as to suggest that reference is being made to the original manuscripts. This effectually deters most readers from following the reference up. It sometimes happens that a writer will give abundant and correct references to support what he has to say about the battle of Hastings or the dissolution of the monasteries or some equally well-known event, while giving none at all for the more striking and unusual incidents in the local scene. Or he will cite a manuscript without saying where he found it ("From a court-roll of the manor we learn" so and so), or without indicating its character ("a manuscript volume in the possession of Mr X"). He will quote a work in many volumes without specifying volume and page. Mr L. J. Ashford, in his otherwise excellent *History of High Wycombe*, goes even further. On p. 285 he quotes an unprinted document with no other reference than the words "Public Record Office." The usefulness of such a footnote can be measured by recalling that the number of documents in that repository, according to the estimate of their official custodians, approximates to fifty million.

What has been said here about references applies also, *mutatis mutandis*, to the index. The obvious course of providing no index at all has many precedents, particularly in the work of foreign scholars. One French academy set out to print and publish the whole series of papal registers, and did actually print about a score of them; but for all the use they have been to students they might just as well have remained unpublished, for hardly any of them are indexed. The concept of an index, in fact, as we understand the term, has found no secure lodging in the Gallic mind. But in this country we like our books to have an index; so it may be as well to make a show of giving the reader what he wants. One sure method of letting him down is to get your wife or a friend to make the index for you. Another is to give about fifty page-references under one entry, without any classification or subdivision. The entries may be confined to personal names, omitting place-names; or *vice versa*. These are the more obvious inadequacies. A really subtle practitioner will improve upon them. The index he provides will look exhaustive, will in fact be so in all the minor entries, and only prolonged use will reveal that some of the most important references are missing. For a crowning touch, he can add a note apologizing for any shortcomings, like the writer who at the end of five hundred closely printed pages gave what he rightly called a "limited index" and explained that it was "prepared under somewhat difficult conditions on board the *Queen Mary* between Southampton and New York."

I have left to the last the most important matter of all. Hutchins, writing a monumental history of Dorset in 1773, remarked: "Works of this kind are of all others least capable of any advantages of

style." How wholeheartedly most local historians
have agreed with Hutchins on that point is plain for
all to see. Moreover, in these days, when a torrent of
letterpress roars past us day and night in full spate,
and every other sentence is an outrage against one
literary canon or another, it is easy enough to write
badly: a bad style is in the very air we breathe. It
does not take long to discover that one grand object
of the contemporary prose-writer is NEVER TO USE
ONE WORD WHERE YOU CAN POSSIBLY USE FOUR.
A single illustration will suffice. I quote it from a
meritorious recent work on suburban history. The
writer wished to make the point that if a speculative
builder believed house-building likely to bring in
fat dividends, he might be tempted to build too
many houses; if not, he would build few or none.
Our historian put it in this way: "The profitability
of house-building, and therefore of the supply of
new houses, depended among other things on the
alternative earnings of the capital used in it, and this
meant that the provision of suburban houses could
either be retarded for lack of capital which had been
put to more profitable employment elsewhere; or,
conversely, it could be expanded far beyond current
needs when idle capital was put to what was considered safe use."

It will be noticed that the structure of this passage rests upon a foundation of impersonal abstract
nouns. The figure of the moneyed man, contemplat-
ing his swollen bank-balance and pondering how
best to employ his spare cash, is completely hidden
from view under a cloud of verbiage. This too is in
strict accordance with contemporary practice. A
crude statement, such as "Balbus built a wall," is

not acceptable in this day and age. Anything sooner than give the impression that history is concerned with human beings. The living, breathing Balbus, the fellow-creature with a mind of his own, must be got rid of at all costs, reduced to a statistical abstraction, an economic trend. The historian who consistently adheres to this great principle may well find it leading him on to higher things. He may end by quitting the lowly plane of history for good and soaring into the empyrean of Sociology, a subject, incidentally, which is much better endowed.

No one who can drive a pen or bang a typewriter should find any difficulty in following the simple precepts enunciated in the foregoing pages. And though success in any literary undertaking is not a thing which can be guaranteed, I believe there is a fair chance of it for the local historian who faithfully and consistently applies the principles I have ventured to lay down for his guidance. If he does this, he can be reasonably confident that his work will be as uninviting to the general reader as exasperating to the well-informed, and that when it has joined the older local histories on the shelves, it will gather as much dust as any of them.

THE PLACE OF TEAM-WORK
IN LOCAL HISTORY

By V. H. T. Skipp

I FIRST became actively interested in local history eleven years ago, in 1955, when I was appointed head of the History Department at a new Birmingham Comprehensive School. I decided that I would like to introduce some local history into the syllabus—not just the history of Birmingham, I thought, but also something about Sheldon, where the school itself was situated, and where most of the children lived. In the present century Sheldon has become a mere suburb of Birmingham, but for a thousand years before that it had existed as a separate little village, a local community in its own right. The medieval parish church was still there. So were the manor-house, the village school, two of the village inns, and several black and white farmhouses and cottages. I wanted to get the children looking at these survivals from the past in their own neighbourhood and learning to make sense of them.

Unfortunately I could find out very little *myself* about the history of Sheldon. Apart from a not very helpful account in the Victoria County History, and a few cursory references elsewhere, nothing appeared to have been written about the place.

On the other hand, visits to the County Record Office at Warwick, the Birmingham Reference Library, and, above all, to the parish church, with its well-stocked parish chest—these visits soon proved that there was no shortage of original source material.

I decided that the only thing to do was to write my own local history. However, I had not got far before it became obvious that if I was going to rely exclusively on my own spare-time labours, this task would take a very long time indeed. My pupils, I thought, would have left school, married, and produced children of their own, before I had much to tell them about the history of Sheldon. It was then that an alternative occurred to me: what was needed was to tackle the work, not on my own, but with the help of a group.

To begin with I tried this approach with my school historical society. But its members were all under thirteen, and although considerable progress was made in some directions, the difficulties of undertaking other aspects of the work with such young children soon became apparent. So in 1957, under the auspices of the Extramural Department of Birmingham University, I started the 'Discovering Sheldon' research course with adults.

Thirty-five people enrolled on the first evening, and twenty-nine of them were still with me when work was concluded three years later, with a specially built travelling exhibition and the publication of a brief parish history.[1] In 1960 new 'Discovering' classes were opened to cover four parishes adjacent to Sheldon, namely Bickenhill, Elmdon, Solihull, and Yardley. Of these the Bickenhill course has already been completed, again with an exhibition

[1] V. H. T. Skipp, *Discovering Sheldon*, Department of Extramural Studies, University of Birmingham, 1960.

and the publication of a parish history.[1] This means that at the present time a compact block of five adjoining north-Warwickshire parishes have been, or are being, brought under scrutiny, the area involved amounting to rather more than 26,000 acres.

These 'Discovering' courses, which are all under my own direction, have been planned on uniform lines. The intention in each case is to study, as far as the limitations of time and material will allow, the development of a local community over the centuries in all its aspects, topographical, economic, social, political, cultural.

We also hope that when the individual parish histories are finished we shall be able to prepare several comparative studies—a discussion of the agrarian history of the area from the Anglo-Saxon settlement to the present day; an analytical examination of over three hundred local inventories which have already been transcribed; a study of poor law administration in the area, and so on.

Now I realize that this kind of project could only be carried out in highly favourable circumstances, such as one finds in big cities and conurbations. In Birmingham we enjoy many advantages which— though they can hardly be unique—are not necessarily found elsewhere.

In the first place, we have no recruitment difficulties whatever. We get the numbers that an extensive project requires, and we also get the right quality of student—people with a good general academic background. My Sheldon group included

[1] V. H. T. Skipp and R. P. Hastings, *Discovering Bickenhill*, Department of Extramural Studies, University of Birmingham, 1963.

twelve schoolteachers. Three had degrees in History, and just as usefully, one had a degree in Geography. In addition there was a works manager, an engineer, and an accountant. On other courses I have had various other types of business people, a solicitor, a farm bailiff, a professional photographer, a journalist, a doctor.

Another respect in which we are lucky at Birmingham is that, on the whole, we find it fairly easy to get hold of the documentary material that is required. In every case, the contents of the parish chest have been made available by the incumbent, though this has meant holding meetings in the church, or in some adjacent building—not always the warmest or most comfortable of places in mid-winter.

Provided we observe certain safeguards, both the Birmingham Reference Library and the Warwick Record Office have been prepared to arrange long-term loans of some types of documents—deed collections, Poor Law Union minutes, parochial records. With other material this is not possible, but then we make a series of visits to the repository itself, if necessary on Saturday mornings.

For documents at the Public Record Office, and other central archives, the University provides a generous annual allowance, so that photostats and microfilms may be obtained. For projecting microfilm we use an ordinary film-strip projector, supplied by the University.

Every 'Discovering' course begins with a series of lectures to initiate people into the work. But thereafter we break down into a number of small research teams, each engaged in a particular aspect of the overall study: for example, population, the topography of the parish, place- and field-names, the care of the poor.

At the end of each year's work, reports of the various investigations are put into duplicated form for distribution to members; and it is on the basis of these reports that the parish history is ultimately written.

The reports are often lengthy, containing far more material than finds its way into the history; so that each course produces about a hundred pages of typescript each year. We do the typing ourselves, but the Extra mural Department undertakes the duplicating, as well as providing paper and duplicating skins. The University is also prepared to finance the publication of the histories and pay for the building of exhibitions. Money from the sale of the books goes back to the University, the price being so arranged that a sell-out produces a small profit.

Finally, being on the doorstep of the University, we are well placed for extra-tutorial help. If good work is to be done, it is important that students should be fed with plenty of general background material, particularly on the social and economic sides. Accompanying the research sessions, therefore, we run a series of lecture meetings and some of these are addressed by University lecturers, speaking on a wide range of specialist topics, stimulating the students, and gradually opening up the wider perspectives which are so essential in local work.

Here, then, are some of the ways in which team-work in local history is 'featherbedded' in Birmingham. In remote rural areas few or none of these advantages may obtain; in which case, local projects may have to be correspondingly less ambitious. This does not mean that, in their own way, they may not still be well worth doing. At the same time I would like to urge that where wider opportunities exist, local groups should attempt work which is as advanced and as ambitious as possible.

This brings me to the central issue: What is the *place* of team-work in the writing of local history?

My own view is that it ought to occupy an extremely important place. Indeed, I would go so far as to suggest that the future progress and development of local history itself could well be seriously inhibited unless ways and means are found of utilizing the tremendous reserves of amateur interest and amateur talent which we all of us know to be available.

In some respects what is happening in local history today seems not dissimilar from what happened in archaeology about a hundred years ago. I realize that, for all sorts of reasons, it would be dangerous to press this analogy too far. Nevertheless, provided we bear in mind that it *is* only an analogy, it may help us to appreciate—more starkly than we could perhaps do otherwise—what is the actual situation in local history at the present time.

In the middle of the nineteenth century, a salutary revolution was taking place in the study of archaeology. Before this, from all accounts, archaeology had been little more than a kind of treasure-hunt indulged in by the squire, the parson, and the local gentry. When you dug, you dug for gold—or at least for some rare and tangible artefact.

Then, in the second half of the nineteenth century, a new and more serious concept of the subject began to gain ground. The purpose was no longer to dig merely for artefacts, but rather, by careful observation and recording, to reconstruct the whole history of the site being excavated—with the additional aim, beyond this, of finding out as much as possible about the people who had built the structure, and lived there. Henceforward plans and sections and soil samples were just as important as things for the mantelpiece—or even for the museum. A post-hole or a drain could evoke as much enthusiasm as a gold stater or the most exquisitely proportioned pot.

Now, like the old-style archaeology, local history in the past used to be very much the prerogative of the parson and the squire. Moreover, it was essentially a treasure-hunt. The gold in this case was a fastidiously documented descent of the manor; a family pedigree going back to the Conquest—often not so fastidiously documented; the history of the family coat of arms. Meanwhile, as in the old archaeology, the actual site of the treasure was largely ignored. That is to say, there was an almost total neglect of the history of the local community itself.

Happily, over the last few decades—and thanks especially to the teaching of the Leicester school— all this has begun to change, so that now, at last, a new concept of local history is gradually establishing itself which is characterized by infinitely wider aims.

The concern today is not only with the descent of the manor and the fortunes of the local big families, but also, and equally, with the history of the husbandman, the village craftsman, the cottager, and the pauper down the centuries. And with the history of the place itself—its changing landscape, its fields, its industries, its lanes, its houses. The aim, in short, is nothing less than to reconstruct the full history of the town or village: to produce, as it were, the biography of a community.

To the extent to which all this is true, local history is currently emerging, almost, one might say, as an entirely new field of study—just as archaeology emerged as a new field of study about a century ago.

So far the parallel I have drawn relates to aims. But I would suggest that, associated with this, there is a second and equally important analogy, this time regarding method.

Because of the ambitious nature of its objectives, and the enormous amount of work entailed in their pursuit, the new archaeology had to train and utilize large numbers of amateur workers. What archaeologist would dream of excavating a Roman settlement on his own? Clearly, this is work for a team of people; some of them, it is to be hoped, almost as experienced and skilled as the directing archaeologist himself, others mere novices.

And surely—to a considerable extent, and for similar reasons—this is the situation with the new local history. Only those who have tried to work through the Leicester formula—to reconstruct the history of a local community in *all* its aspects, from its foundation down to the present day—only those who have tried to do this can have any idea of the amount of work that is involved.

Let me give an example. One of the first jobs we do when we start work on a parish is to take the mid-nineteenth-century tithe map and award and produce from this a series of four maps: one, showing the land-ownership about 1840; a second, the land occupation—the farms; a third showing land utilization—arable, pasture, or meadow; and a fourth showing all the field-names.

This series of maps, when completed, gives a really thorough understanding of the topography and the tenurial situation in the parish as it was a little over a hundred years ago. Because of the tendency for field-names and—quite often—ownership and occupation units to persist unchanged over the centuries, these maps also provide an ideal basis from which to begin working out the medieval topography. I would hesitate myself to tackle a local research without the tithe award behind me, and without producing these four maps from it.

But consider the work that is involved. The largest of our parishes, Solihull, has over 3,000 fields. To make and colour the four maps took a team of eight people a full year of course time, that is to say, forty-eight hours. The inference is that one research worker would have taken not far short of four hundred, or, on the basis of a forty-hour week, ten weeks.

Or take population. In all but one of our parishes, before we could *start* population work, it was necessary to transcribe the complete baptismal register at the very least. Again, here is a year's course time, for anything from six to ten people, depending on the size of the parish. And these are just a couple of the preliminary jobs. Relatively speaking, they don't amount to much more than the archaeologist stripping off his turf.

In his preface to *Discovering Bickenhill*, Professor

Finberg estimated that the task of producing that book would have taken a solitary historian anything up to five years, if he could have given his whole time to it; and anything up to ten if he had pursued it in the intervals of other work. The group had completed and published its research in the space of three.

Some may feel that speed is no recommendation. If standards were in jeopardy, this would indeed be true. But I am postulating an efficiently organized and professionally controlled type of research in which standards are not in jeopardy. Furthermore, there are over ten thousand ancient parishes in this country, all of which, ideally speaking, need studying and re-studying along the lines which are being laid down by modern scholarship. In addition, there is almost limitless scope for wider regional studies. With this kind of future programme, it seems to me that it is in the very logic of the situation that the new local history—like the new archaeology before it—needs to be developed as a group activity.

If amateurs working in groups *are* going to make a significant contribution to the new local history, clearly we have to think of them as organizing themselves in many different ways. The W.E.A. or extramural class, about which I am mostly speaking, is only one of them, though probably it is better suited than any other for the comprehensive investigation of individual local communities, for the writing of town and village histories.

Another type of organization which has much useful work before it is the local history society. As well as the part such bodies play in fostering general interest in the subject, they are admirably placed to promulgate regional and county studies of various kinds. One thinks, for instance, of the piece of work done by the East Yorkshire Local History Society on 'Parish Registers and Illiteracy in East Yorkshire.' From 1754 marriage registers required the newly-weds either to sign their names or, if they could not write, to make their marks. By counting the marks and signatures year by year it is possible to form some idea of the progress of literacy. Individual members of the East Yorkshire Society worked on different parish registers and counted the marks and signatures. Then this material was collated centrally and the results were written up and published in pamphlet form.

Literally dozens of useful surveys could be carried out in a similar way. Nor would this kind of work in any sense quarrel with the parochial studies being undertaken by local groups. On the contrary, it would greatly aid and augment them. The more regional publications there are available, the easier it is for the local group to place its own town or village in its proper context and perspective.

Yet another possibility is the organizing of group work on a national scale. The recently launched Cambridge Demographic Research project represents a pioneer effort of this kind; and it is feasible that the Standing Conference for Local History could encourage similar nation-wide investigations through its County Committees.

So far I have been stressing the enormous future scope for team-work in local history. Before concluding, I ought perhaps to mention some of the requirements which need to be met, and some of the difficulties which will have to be overcome, if such team-work is to be really successful and effective.

One of the most urgent needs is to discover and train suitable research directors. Everywhere the demand for local history research courses greatly exceeds the supply of tutors. Not only that, but many of the tutors who are being used by the W.E.A. and extramural Departments have little understanding of how to tackle local projects.

In a good number of classes, nothing more is attempted than the transcription of documents for its own sake. In others, some effort is made to extract facts, but because the tutor himself lacks the necessary background and judgement, he is unable to instil these qualities in his students. The result is that everyone is overwhelmed by the sheer bulk of material—and either nothing is written up at all, or, if it is, what results is an exceedingly ill-conceived, ill-digested, and amorphous compilation.

The day is past—or ought to be past—when a bit of palaeography, a bit of medieval Latin, and a 'manors and castles' interest in local history, fitted people to conduct research courses in this subject. As Professor Finberg emphasizes, the new local history is a highly advanced and complex discipline.[1] If we accept this, surely it must ultimately be the task of the universities to train professionals in this sphere—as they already train professional archaeologists. Until more universities follow Leicester's example and accept this responsibility, far too many local groups are bound to languish and falter for want of proper guidance.

Closely associated with the need for fully trained

[1] page 44.

research directors there is the need to work out and perfect a whole series of basic techniques for use in the various branches of the subject.

Each community is unique and will present its own difficulties and problems. At the same time, many of the issues that need to be investigated are common ones. How do you estimate population totals before the first decennial census? What dangers and pitfalls have to be avoided in endeavouring to do so? How can an assessment be made from the parish registers of the extent of immigration and emigration at various times? How can you estimate the expectation of life in former centuries? How do you set about systematically reconstructing the medieval topography of a village by the use of the mid-nineteenth-century tithe award and medieval deed material?

Once methods have been worked out and disseminated for tackling these and the many other problems, amateurs will have little difficulty in applying them. Archaeology has only been able to use amateur workers to the extent that it has because it has got its own basic techniques firmly established. In local history, as in archaeology, the existence of standard techniques will ensure, not merely that the right questions are asked, but also that they are answered in the right way and with the proper safeguards. Indeed, on the level of data collection and analysis these techniques should do much of the amateur's thinking for him. At the same time, scope will always be left for an original and creative response to the material, particularly when the time comes for synthesis and presentation.

Good research directors, good techniques; the other thing required is good amateur workers.

Here the recruitment of suitable people is important, but still more important perhaps is to cut down the *wastage* of *experienced* amateurs; to try to see that once people have been trained they are not lost to the work.

What happens, all too often, is that adult students take part in one local research, lasting two or three years—and by the end of it they really are beginning to get to grips with the disciplines involved. Unfortunately, that *is* the end of it. Either there is no second course for them to join—or else, if there is, they lack the inclination to join it.

We have found with the 'Discovering' classes that one of the great merits of studying a block of parishes is that students are able to pass on to a second and even a third course. Twenty-one of the twenty-nine finishers at Sheldon joined the Bickenhill, Elmdon, Solihull, or Yardley groups. Half a dozen of them joined at two places. This meant that when we started these new courses we already had a sizeable nucleus of trained people who could help the others to pick up the work. Ten of my students are now in their ninth year with me; three have assisted from time to time with tutorial work.

It is possible that this idea of studying a group of parishes could help towards building up effective research teams in rural areas, particularly if the initial class were put on at a place which was reasonably populous and where one could be sure of getting a good initial recruitment.

Of course, left to themselves, many amateurs would have no inclination to join a second research.

Most of them don't start off with a *general* interest in local history; they start with a *particular* interest in their own town or village. Before they will want to study another local community, apart from their own, this excessive parochialism has to be overcome, and their perspectives widened. But then that ought to be one of the objects of a good local history course in any case.

Lastly, what about the serious practical difficulties that at present beset many local groups? I refer to things like the difficulty of gaining access to documents, financing publications, and so on.

My own belief is that these problems will gradually be overcome as the level of work done by amateur groups is improved, as public appreciation of this work increases, and as academic opinion learns to take the new local history more seriously.

A remarkable extension of archive services has occurred over the last twenty years, and if public interest continues to grow, the future may see still more being done to improve the availability of documentary material. Microfilm and photostat facilities might be further extended—perhaps on a loan basis. Better staffed, the record offices would no doubt be prepared to accommodate adult groups in the evenings. Even a mobile archive service could conceivably be developed, so that in rural areas the mountain could go to Mohammed.

Similarly, as the new local history gathers momentum, the universities, trusts of various kinds, even perhaps local government authorities, may show an increasing readiness to supply the comparatively modest financial assistance that local groups require.

In all these matters, we have to remember that it is still early days. The tenets of the Leicester school were not fully enunciated until 1952. It was not until the early 'fifties that the pioneer adult education groups began their researches; their publications have only been appearing for about ten years. Obviously this has not been long enough to overcome all the practical difficulties. Nor would it be reasonable to expect that the techniques of team-work have yet been perfected. Nevertheless, I imagine that most professional historians who are interested in local history would agree that this movement has made a promising start. However right or wrong I may have been in my detailed assessments and prognostications, I am myself convinced that it has before it an extremely promising future.

THE USE OF LOCAL HISTORY IN THE SCHOOLS

By V. H. T. Skipp

I

O N an earlier page Professor Finberg quoted the Board of Education circular which as long ago as 1908 argued that the best approach to the teaching of British history in secondary schools was by means of local material.[1] The Ministry pamphlet *Teaching History*, published in 1952, still urges the use of "particular" and "concrete" local material, claiming that it helps to set "the pupils' minds and imagination to work," and makes the history lesson more "vivid by illustration."[2]

Many teachers have ignored such recommendations, but some have been keen to implement them, with the result that, in one form or another, a fair amount of local material has percolated into the classroom. There are signs that over the last decade the number of the converted has been increasing. At the same time, even the most ardent exponents of the local approach seem in little danger of carrying it too far. Most secondary schools are committed to courses in British history, usually with some European and World history as well. In these circumstances all practising teachers would agree with the Ministry that the rôle of local history must

[1] page 25.
[2] *Teaching History*, H.M.S.O., p. 54.

inevitably remain ancillary as far as curricular work is concerned. Apart perhaps from the occasional short project, there can be little question of studying it for its own sake; its purpose, rather, must be to provide "a storehouse of examples" with which to illustrate and illuminate the broad national story.

If this is to be the position, it follows that any piece of local material, in order to win a place in the syllabus, will have to satisfy two basic requirements. First, it must be strictly relevant to the course concerned: by which I mean that it must provide subject-matter for a theme or topic which it has been considered desirable to include on entirely independent grounds. Secondly, the local material must be intrinsically worth while and interesting. The teacher should not have the feeling at the back of his mind that, merely on the grounds of locality, it is keeping out more trenchant or significant material from other parts.

It is no part of my intention to urge the use of local history beyond these orthodox bounds. The point I wish to make rather is that, *within those bounds*, a great deal more useful material is available than the majority of teachers have yet realized.

Paradoxically, the tardiness of the profession in this regard may to some extent be due to the 1908 circular; for it could be argued that local history in the schools got away to a false, because premature, start. Certainly its early advocates, we can now see, were operating within an extremely limited range. They tended to think of local history largely in terms of important national events that happened to have occurred in a particular locality, or of fortuitous local associations with nationally important people. And in truth, the town and parish histories which were current in their time offered little else that was of relevance to general history. (The descent of the manor, the genealogies of prominent local families, the advowson of the church, etc., most certainly were not.) But in recent times there have been important developments in our ideas about the nature and scope of local history; and these in turn have increased enormously the extent to which a teacher can now carry out the 1908 precept: to "make constant reference to the history of the locality as illustrative of the general history."

In the first place, ten years after the publication of *The Making of the English Landscape*, much more use could surely be made of the topographical material that is available in any locality. I know that the universities, unlike some colleges of education, are scarcely as yet encouraging this approach, but I look forward to a time when history teachers will have grown thoroughly accustomed to thinking of the landscape, in the words of Professor Hoskins, as "the richest historical record we possess."[1] Every phase of British history, from prehistoric times onwards, can be illustrated in the field; and it can be illustrated in such a way that it will speak to the deepest part of the student, his imagination.

When it comes to field-work no one will deny that the amount which can be undertaken in school time is severely limited. There is the possibility of evening or Saturday excursions. But I am not thinking

[1] W. G. Hoskins, *The Making of the English Landscape*, Hodder & Stoughton, 1955, p. 14.

exclusively, or even mainly, of organized expeditions. Boys and girls have bikes nowadays; they have cameras; their parents have cars. To a considerable extent, pupils are capable of doing their own field-work. All that is needed is for them to be stimulated by the teacher, and told where the worthwhile places are. The best way of doing this is to be constantly referring to the local landscape and to the fascinating remains that can be seen in it. A series of distribution maps might be prepared, showing Celtic forts, Roman excavations, castles, monastic ruins, parish church architecture of various periods, brasses and stone effigies, country houses, wind and water mills, historic industrial sites. If these maps are displayed one at a time, at appropriate points in the course, and if the teacher talks about a few of the places, perhaps illustrating what he says with a series of film transparencies, then some of the children will be certain to respond. They will bring back guide books, sketches, plans, photographs, specimens, and these things in turn can be displayed in the history room to stimulate others: and so this habit of using the landscape for history will grow and become a tradition in the school.

Visits to historical monuments and landscape features may take our pupils far afield. But many themes and topics can be illustrated from the immediate locality. Again I feel that not enough is being done to bring into use this immediately local material. In dealing with the medieval open-field system, how many schools take as their illustration their own local open-field system? In dealing with enclosure, how many schools study their own local enclosure award? Are the local turnpike, the local canal, the local railway discussed when the transport revolution is under consideration? In speaking of social life in Tudor and Stuart times are the sixteenth- and seventeenth-century probate inventories of local inhabitants used?

I could go on to ask another fifty questions of this kind. And in each case an affirmative answer would mean that an additional piece of significant and intrinsically useful local material had found its way into the classroom. Much of it, it is true, would have relevance mainly in courses where a good deal of social and economic history is taught. But in such courses—if there is time, and if the necessary information can be discovered—a very considerable body of local history could be included in the schemes without in any sense ceasing to teach general history, or departing from the reservations referred to above concerning the use of local material.

Moreover, it should not be forgotten that this local approach is itself putting over an important point about the past. Our modern way of life, dominated as it is by the welfare state, by instant communications, world-wide horizons, and ad-mass culture, is fundamentally different from anything which preceded it. Before the advent of the railway, the internal combustion engine, the penny daily, the telephone, wireless, and television, almost all experience was localized: the town or village was the vessel which shaped people's lives. The same tendency towards localization obtained in matters of government and public administration. So much so, that down to the nineteenth century one might almost say that the government did not govern England: England governed itself. The state then was neither omnicompetent nor omnipresent; the parish seemed very nearly both. Even on the eve of Peterloo, Lord Liverpool was quite prepared to leave everything to "the gentlemen of the parish." Admittedly with disastrous consequences, for we now realize that Manchester in 1819 stood on the watershed in this respect. A new society—our own—was on the way: a society which was to alter beyond recognition the very meaning of the word 'parochial'.

Yet for many centuries the local community—borough and manor first, then borough and parish—provided the basic framework for the administrative, economic, and social evolution of the nation. From which it follows that if one wishes to illustrate properly any of these aspects of national history, one is compelled, sooner or later, to come down to the local units. Even the textbooks, in so far as they depart from generalized statements, are compelled to do so. They will be quoting, let us say, from the records of Essex or Oxfordshire. Where comparable material can be discovered on one's own doorstep, one is surely sacrificing little and gaining much by making use of it.

When speaking of the condition of the roads in the seventeenth and eighteenth centuries, what better than to quote from the accounts of the Surveyors of the Highways? Before the advent of macadamized surfaces, these accounts consist chiefly of payments made for loads of stones and gravel to fill up the ruts and holes:

The Accounts of Joseph Field Surveyor of the Highways in the Parish of Sheldon for the Year 1779.

P[ai]d Tho[ma]s Tatton for Stones	0	2	6
63 Loads of Gravel	1	1	0
24 Loads of Stones		12	0

. . . . . .

For 8 Loads of Rubbish		3	0
Thomas Tatton for Work		2	0
Drink		5	0
32 Loads of Stones		16	0
Drink		5	0

To slip in brief local illustrations like this need take little time, yet they can help to make history a living subject. For locality is to history what topicality is to journalism. Of itself the material may be nothing exceptional. But the 'here' seems to add somehow to its sharpness and relevance. The examples I am choosing are quite arbitrary, but when touching on the health of former generations and the history of medicine, the local doctor's bills from the Sheldon parish chest have always seemed to me worth quoting. Here is an extract from one dated 1746:

July 8	A Vomit for your Daughter	6d.
	Purging Salts	3d.
10	Cordial Drops	6d.
15	Bleeding your Daughter	6d.
	Purging Salts	3d.
	Bleeding your Self	6d.
16	The Drops	6d.

When dealing with the Poor Law, need we be content with bald textbook summaries of the important statutes? If they are obtainable, could not the local Overseers' Accounts be used to illustrate the Poor Law in action? Let me demonstrate the kind of material that is frequently available under this head by outlining a typical pauper case history built up from the Sheldon Overseers' Accounts and other parochial documents.

At the beginning of 1766, the Hodgetts were a family of seven. Their people had been in the parish for about a century; once they had held land, for a Hodgetts Close is among the field-names. John Hodgetts himself appears to have been a day labourer, but by the mid-1750's his wages must have been insufficient to support a growing family, and he begins drawing semi-regular relief—Necessity Money, payments for clothes, etc. For example, in 1757–8 he receives money and goods to the value of £4 from the parish: an appreciable sum at a time when the schoolmaster's salary was a mere £5 per annum.

Then in February, 1766, the breadwinner dies. In the accounts for that year is the entry: "Feb. 4. Jon hoghits had 3 poynts of wine—2s. 6d." This was to ease him over his last hours. There follows: "Feb. 8. Pd hoghits furnel all Charges—£1."

Mrs Hodgetts and her five children are now solely dependent on the parish. They are paid Necessity Money, averaging at first about six shillings per week. A fortnight after the father's funeral, however, Katherine, the youngest child, is buried. Necessity Money is now reduced to between three and four shillings, though the family also receive quite a lot of help in kind:

Feb. 23. Pd for 6 hundred of coal for the Widow hoghits
                                                        4s. od.
March 5. Bo[ugh]t the widow hoghits half a peck of Beanes
                                                        1s. 2d.
Apl. 15. Hodgetts had a pare of Briches   1s. 6d.

Unfortunately, the Overseers were not prepared to go on subsidizing the family to this extent indefinitely; and the only way to escape doing so was by placing the children out as apprentices. Accordingly, on 15th May, William, the eldest boy, aged ten, is bound to William Rothwell, a steel-snuffer maker of Birmingham. In July, Hannah, aged twelve, goes to Arley—twenty miles away—to serve Thomas Lee in husbandry. By now Necessity Money is down to 6d. per week: the parish is being "saved harmless."

At the beginning of October, the Widow Hodgetts herself dies. On the day of the funeral, after the burial fees, there is the pathetic entry: "Bread for the Children—5d."

The following March, the last remaining boy is apprenticed. Thirteen months only have elapsed since the death of the father. Yet of a family of seven, only Elizabeth, the eldest girl, remains in Sheldon. During the next ten years she presents the Overseers with two illegitimate children.

Now a story like this really does throw some light on the workings of the old Poor Law. And it is marvellous classroom material. Not only will it evoke the imaginative sympathy of the children, but it can be used to set them thinking too. For instance, by question and answer, the contrast between this system and our modern system of social security can be elicited from the pupils. Had John

Hodgetts fallen ill today, instead of his "3 poynts of wine," he would have been whisked away into hospital and cared for, free of charge, under the National Health Service. Very probably he would not have died. Had he done so, the Widow Hodgetts would have had a widow's pension, together with child allowances; and, if these proved inadequate, she could have applied for National Assistance. Instead of the children being apprenticed and sent away from home, they would have stayed with their mother and continued their education.

This is an effective story in any case; but I do not think I am guilty of overstatement when I say that teaching in a Sheldon school, I have found it at least fifty per cent more effective than it would have been had the Hodgetts lived elsewhere and the story come out of a textbook. Apart from which fact, one can by no means be certain of finding such stories in textbooks. In the local records themselves they abound.

Why, then, with such excellent material available, is the local approach still making so little headway in the schools? Partly it is due to shortage of teaching time. But, as I have already said, the extra time involved need not be excessive. Besides, what is generally lamented as a shortage of time can, from another point of view, be just as truthfully described as an overcrowding of the history syllabus. In which case, at least in the pre-examination years, there is nothing to stop the teacher from doing a little pruning. There is nothing to stop him either from considering what kind of history really interests the child. "It used to infuriate me," writes W. G. Hoskins, "to see my eleven-year-old daughter grappling with 'subjects' like Castlereagh's foreign policy, but knowing nothing of the history of the Oxfordshire parish in which we then lived, of the fact, for example, that in the field next to our own garden there lay the visible remains of the 'lost' medieval village of Steeple Barton. No wonder so many grown-ups loathe the very word 'history'."[1]

I myself do quite a lot of lecturing to 'grown-ups' nowadays. I have one lecture on the development of Birmingham in which, among other things, I try to put across the idea that the modern city contains over forty buried villages and hamlets, each of which had anything up to a thousand years of separate and independent history before it was eventually swallowed up by the expanding 'wen': not, needless to say, without leaving conspicuous traces behind. This idea comes to many of my listeners with the force of a revelation, and, time and time again, their response is the same: "Why weren't we taught this kind of history when we were at school?" I submit that, in the incidental way I have tried to indicate, their sons and daughters should be.

In the upper forms of secondary schools the present examination system does much to retard the introduction of local material. The most favoured G.C.E. papers, being almost entirely political, offer little scope for it. In any case, where the stereotyped answer is felt to be the best, because safest, way of ensuring success, anything which lacks the authority of the textbook tends to be excluded as suspect, if not positively dangerous. At my own school we took the Oxford Social and Eco-

[1] Preface to John West, *Village Records*, Macmillan, 1962, p. viii.

nomic 'O' level paper and I encouraged pupils to use apposite local material wherever possible. My successor reversed this policy. When pupils had recourse to local illustrations in their essays, he scrawled in the margin, "Not relevant to National History." Incidentally, I recently met a product of the 'safe' method who is now in his third year at university. On asking him how he was getting on, he replied, "Not too badly. I think I'm just beginning to understand history instead of learning it." A few months from tripos seems rather late in the day to be making such a disturbing confession. Is it too much to hope that this examination-induced travesty which still passes for successful history teaching will one day pass from our midst? Perhaps not. Some C.S.E. papers are already offering scope for a more satisfying and meaningful approach; and maybe, as happens so often in education, the process of re-thinking is destined to spread from below upwards. If so, the use of local history in the schools is likely to spread with it.

Another withholding factor is that the sources of local history are still largely unknown to teachers. I came down from Cambridge without realizing that such a thing as the Parish Chest existed, or at least that it might contain anything of interest to the *serious* historian. As for our "richest historical record," an Oxford graduate who had been commissioned to write a textbook on British medieval history recently expressed astonishment when I explained to her that the visible remains of the medieval open fields are still to be traced all over the midland landscape. The widespread failure of the universities even to introduce potential teachers to the topographical and documentary sources of local history is surely one more argument—to be added to a good many others—in favour of establishing independent university departments which are devoted to this aspect of historical studies, along the lines of that at Leicester.

Before leaving the subject of curricular teaching, let me draw together my remarks by considering briefly what might be the overall pattern of the local content in a school history syllabus. I suggest that ideally a school would avail itself both of the history of the region in which it is situated and that of its own township. Certain periods and themes it will be difficult to illustrate otherwise than regionally. As a rule, this would apply to the prehistoric, Roman, and Anglo-Saxon periods. Thereafter, the teacher could continue to etch in the regional picture if only by describing the characteristic topographical remains. But from Domesday times onwards, it should be possible to handle many subjects from the actual place where the school is situated. Thus, the emergence of the feudal system by 1086 could be illustrated by giving pupils a 'feudal ladder' derived from the local Domesday entry; the manorial system by quoting the local court rolls, and saying whatever it is possible to say about the layout of the local manor, the site of the manor-house, and so on.

According to this framework, the region would be quarried for archaeological and topographical material, whereas the use of the documentary record would be restricted mainly to one's own town or village.

At least, this might be so until the mid-eighteenth

century: with the Industrial Revolution and the approach of modern times, the canvas ought again to be widened. In the West Midlands, the teacher would probably want to take as his local theme the development of the Black Country and the rise of Birmingham.

For the most part the local material would be put over by means of brief oral intrusions. Occasionally, however, time might be found for students to undertake a short research exercise. With very little trouble, a school could obtain photo-copies of forty probate inventories of local inhabitants in Tudor and Stuart times. Transcriptions would have to be made and attached to the photo-copies. Then, at an appropriate point in the course, each child could be handed an inventory—photo-copy plus transcription—and asked to discover from it how many rooms there were in the house, what the rooms were called, how they were furnished, and, by inference, how they were used. It might be possible for them to produce a diagram indicating the layout. They could also ascertain what crops the yeoman or husbandman was cultivating, how many cattle, pigs, and sheep he kept, what farm implements he had at his disposal, what crafts were carried on in the home. When each pupil had studied his own inventory, the project could be rounded off by a class discussion, relating and comparing the findings.[1]

At a later stage, similar exercises could be based

[1] For further information on probate inventories and their use, see West, *Village Records*, pp. 92–131; F. G. Emmison, *Archives and Local History*, pp. 48–49, and 91–94; F. W. Steer, *Probate Inventories*, Historical Association, Short Guide to Records No. 3.

on extracts from the Overseers' accounts, on a series of apprenticeship indentures, or of examination certificates, with their brief but illuminating biographies of the labouring poor.[1] Sometimes a lesson or homework might be devoted to field-work in the town or village concerned: visiting a moated site, tracing the line of an old road, walking along a section of the local canal, or identifying the houses which survive from a particular period.

A number of C.S.E. Boards allow candidates to submit an individual local study for examination purposes. Pupils who had received the kind of introduction I have suggested, both to the local historical background and to some of the simpler techniques of research, would be well fitted to avail themselves of this attractive and enlightened option.

II

Not one place in a hundred yet has anything approaching an adequate parish history, so that the teacher who wishes to bring his immediately local material into circulation will very likely find that the only way of doing so is by mounting his own research. However, it is possible to turn this difficulty into a positive advantage since such work can provide an interesting and valuable field of activity for a school historical society.

[1] On apprenticeship indentures, see W. E. Tate, *The Parish Chest*, Cambridge University Press, 1946, pp. 220–5; on examination certificates, *ibid.*, pp. 201–3. For a remarkable example of a county authority encouraging the use of photo-copies of local records in its schools, see E. R. Lloyd, 'The use of Historical Documents in Schools,' *The Amateur Historian*, Vol. VII, No. 2, pp. 47–52.

Supposing a teacher wishes to tackle a local research project, how can he best set about doing it? There are, of course, dozens of ways; but there is one golden rule that must always be borne in mind. Whatever he does, the teacher must not start without a plan, without a clear objective in mind. The secret of this work is to ask questions. Decide to begin with the kind of things you would like to find out about the place you are studying; formulate these curiosities as questions; then set about systematically collecting all the facts that will enable you to answer the questions. In this way you will always retain control of your material. You will not be inundated by facts. Nor will you be in danger of imitating countless earlier local historians who made a heap of all they knew. An appetite for information is not enough in this kind of work. What is rather more important is the capacity for digestion.

Some teachers may decide to begin by doing research into a specific and limited topic, like the local enclosure award, or the local turnpike road. Others —particularly if they have at their disposal a sizeable historical society—may be brave enough to embark on a more general study of their town or village. Obviously each school must tailor its programme to its own resources and requirements. If it is at all possible, though, there is much to be said for an all-round approach. Not only will this be exciting in itself; it will also ensure that you arrive at a thorough and comprehensive understanding of the place in question, thereby giving your teaching of local material a richness and depth which might otherwise be lacking.

I am going to assume that what you will be studying is a parish, which, if we exclude the corporate towns, was normally the basic unit of the old English community: not only ecclesiastically, but also, from Tudor times to the nineteenth century, for most secular purposes.

In studying your local parish, then, the question I suggest you might ask to begin with is: What was this place like to live in about a hundred years ago?

Now this big question will immediately suggest subsidiary ones. First, a hundred or so years ago, what was it like in appearance? The document that will help you to answer this question is the mid-nineteenth-century tithe map and award. This is generally dated about 1840 and was made when tithes in kind were commuted into money charges on land. Most parishes, though not all, will be found to possess this document, and there should be three copies in existence: a parish copy (probably in the vestry or the parsonage), a diocesan copy at the diocesan record office, and a third copy with the Tithe Redemption Commission, Finsbury Square, London.

The tithe map is an accurate, large-scale survey which shows every individual field or plot of land, as well as all roads, buildings, and boundaries. Accompanying it should go the tithe apportionment, which serves it as a schedule.[1]

I would suggest that you have a photostat made of the map: for an average sized parish this would cost £2–£3. You could have the schedule photostated, but this might be rather expensive, and it

[1] For additional information on tithe awards, see West, *Village Records*, pp. 145–57.

I

would not be a terribly long job to take a transcription.

With the photostat of the map and a copy of the schedule, you are ready to start bringing the parish of a hundred years ago to life. On the map every field is numbered; on the schedule, against the number of each plot, you will be given the following information: the name of the landowner, the name of the occupier, the name and description of the land or premises, the state of cultivation (i.e., the land use), the acreage, and the rent-charge apportioned.

Working in pairs, the members of your research group can make four outline tracings of the map. Then the pages of the schedule are circulated amongst them, and one pair takes off all the field-names, ultimately producing a complete field-names map; a second group concentrates on landowners, building up an ownership map; while the third and fourth groups produce occupation and land use maps respectively.

When they have been completed, a great deal of interesting information can be discovered from this series of maps. The ownership map will show how strong economically the local squire was. The occupation map will give you the number and size of the farms and the names of the farmers. The land-use map will reveal what type of farming predominated. Every building in the *c.* 1840 parish will be shown on the tithe map, so a field survey can be instituted to see how many of these survive, and in the case of the more interesting ones a record can be made of them with the aid of drawings and photographs.[1]

[1] See Hoskins, *Local History in England*, Ch. IX.

Gradually you will be able to build up a clear and detailed picture of the topography of the parish as it was in the mid-nineteenth century, as well as establishing some of the essential facts about what in a rural community would have been the most important village industry, farming.

After the landscape, you will probably want to consider the population of the parish as it was about 1840. The most obvious things to make for here are the early directories—the Post Office Directories, White's, Kelly's, etc.,—which should be available at any large library. These directories will give some useful information, followed by a list of the principal inhabitants, including most tradesmen and craftsmen; so that, with the information already gleaned from the tithe award, a general idea of the social and economic structure of the place should begin to emerge.[1]

If you decide to go beyond this, the next thing to get a copy of is the 1841 or the 1851 census return.[2] The 1851 return is more detailed than the 1841 in several respects. On the other hand, if you wish to hold the work together, it is probably best, irrespective of this fact, to choose the return which is nearest in date to the year of your tithe award. The detailed census enumerations are available for every parish at the Public Record Office, and for an average sized place a microfilm copy can be ob-

[1] See Hoskins, *Local History in England*, p. 26; West, *Village Records*, pp. 162–69.

[2] See Hoskins, *Local History in England*, pp. 26–28; M. Beresford, 'The Unprinted Census Returns of 1841, 1851, 1861 for England and Wales,' in *The Amateur Historian*, Vol. v, No. 8, pp. 260–69.

tained postally for from £2 to £5. A microfilm projector is not required; an ordinary filmstrip projector serves admirably.

Using the census, a full occupation analysis of the parish can be prepared. Work can be done on the size and structure of households; on the age structure of the community, and the distribution of the sexes in the various age-groups. You can find out what proportion of children went to school, and over what period of their childhood. With the 1851 census the place of birth of each person is given, so that it is possible to assess the degree of mobility, while a map can be prepared showing where the immigrants came from.

Such a programme of research might keep a school historical society of, say, twenty members pretty fully occupied for a couple of years. The work is by no means too complicated or difficult even for young secondary children, though it does require firm direction and control from the teacher. Incidentally, I know personally of two schools which have produced excellent surveys along these lines.

Once you have gained a good basic understanding of the local community as it was a little over a hundred years ago—and assuming that you are prepared to do still more work—three possible courses will lie open to you.

First, you may decide to fill out your portrait of the parish as it was in the mid-nineteenth century. This can be done by the use of local newspapers, by the study of tombstones in the churchyard, by the questioning of elderly inhabitants.

The parish chest material is likely to be either in the care of the incumbent or else at the county record office. If you can gain access to this, a series of investigations can be carried out on the government of the parish during the early nineteenth century (from the Vestry minutes); on the maintenance of law and order (from the Constable's accounts); on the care of the poor (from the Overseers' accounts); on the upkeep of the highways (from the Surveyors' accounts). Perhaps the nineteenth-century school, or schools, could be investigated; and much interesting work could be done on the parish registers.[1]

The second thing you might decide to do from your basic 1840 cross-section is to trace the history of the community backwards. On the topographical side, you will naturally see whether you can discover any maps of the parish which are earlier than 1840. Perhaps there will be a Parliamentary Enclosure award or a private Enclosure agreement, or you may be lucky enough to find an early estate map.[2]

The sort of questions you will be asking now are as follows. Where were the open fields situated? Where were the ancient dole meadows, and where were the original commons? Where was the manor-house? What were the boundaries of the demesne?

To discuss in detail the various methods which are available for puzzling out the medieval topography of a parish would itself require several lectures. Absolutely basic to this work, however, is the systematic collection of field-names. Often identifications can be made between names occurring in ancient deeds and the tithe map field-names. Thus

[1] W. E. Tate, *The Parish Chest*, is the standard reference work on parochial archives.

[2] See West, *Village Records*, pp. 137–44.

at Sheldon the medieval open field called Elrefurlang in 1226 is clearly to be identified with nine
adjacent enclosures all marked Elder Field on the
1840 map. In this way the position and boundaries
of the thirteenth-century Elrefurlang—otherwise
lost—can be safely conjectured. Then there will be
other 1840 field-names which declare themselves
to be of medieval origin in any case. The field-name
Breach, for instance, derives from the Old English
braec, meaning 'land newly taken into cultivation';
Etchells means 'an addition, something added to
an estate'; Ridding comes from the Old English
hryding, 'a clearing'; Stocking was a Middle English word, meaning 'a clearing of stumps, a piece of
ground cleared of stumps'. A fair scatter of such
names will probably come through to the mid-
nineteenth-century tithe map and they are all valid
clues to the medieval topography of the manor.[1]

Another thing which will need investigation in
this connection is the landscape itself. Medieval
ridge and furrow may survive in some parts of the
parish; elsewhere the aratral curve can perhaps be
traced in the hedgerows. There may be ancient
moated sites, the tumps of old windmills, depres-
sions representing medieval fish-ponds, hollow-
ways, and long forgotten boundary stones to be discovered and recorded.[2]

Alongside this, using the parish registers and

---

[1] On field-names reference might first be made to the volumes
for individual counties published by the English Place-Name
Society; also A. H. Smith, *English Place-Name Elements*, 1956.

[2] See Hoskins, *Local History in England*, Ch. VIII; Ordnance
Survey, *Field Archaeology: Some notes for beginners*, H.M.S.O.,
1963.

any other parochial material which is available, work could proceed on the people of the parish in the earlier centuries. The number of baptisms, marriages, and burials could be counted year by year. By means of the Cox estimate, rough population totals could be worked out and graphed.[1] In the burial registers the ravages of dearth and disease could be investigated, and a study made of infant and child mortality.[2] For houses and home life, and for many intimate details regarding social conditions, the probate inventories discussed earlier provide almost limitless possibilities.

If all this seems a little too forbidding, the third thing you may decide to do from the 1840 cross-section is to trace the history of the community forward, from 1840 down to the present day. This can be particularly interesting in parishes, like Sheldon, which were rural a hundred years ago but have been subject to extensive urbanization since.

Some teachers in town schools might well decide to ignore the rural past altogether, concentrating entirely on the urban history and industrial archaeology of their district. There is ample scope for field-work and systematic recording in this sphere, perhaps undertaken with the help of geographers. Such work would be particularly worth while in areas where widespread redevelopment is taking place and sectors of an earlier townscape are in danger of disappearing without record.[3]

[1] Tate, *The Parish Chest*, p. 81.
[2] See Hoskins, *Local History in England*, Ch. X.
[3] See Kenneth Hudson, *Industrial Archaeology*, John Baker, 1963; id., *Handbook for Industrial Archaeologists*, J. Baker, 1967.

A school which started off with the mid-nine-teenth-century tithe award and census return, then subsequently, one after another, adopted each of the three courses I have suggested, would ultimately have brought together sufficient material for the writing of a full-scale parish history.

I know of one school which has almost got this far. And indeed, given teachers who are capable of appreciating what the new local history is about, who know the right questions to ask, and are pre-pared to familiarize themselves with the sources from which they must be answered; given these—plus almost limitless reserves of time and patience—there is no reason why the occasional school should not produce a perfectly adequate village history.

Nevertheless, in my opinion the ideal unit for undertaking this full-scale venture is not the school but the adult group, like those organized by the W.E.A. and university extramural depart-ments.

Sometimes it may be possible for a school and an adult group to work together. What I have in mind is that the schoolmaster might negotiate the forma-tion of an extramural class in his own district, him-self becoming a member—or perhaps even the tutor—of this group. Suitable aspects of the re-search could then be taken over by him, with a view to getting the work done at school. If the topics chosen were reasonably specific and self-contained, members of the historical society could ultimately write up and duplicate a full report of their findings. They would thus have accomplished something which was complete in itself, at the same time mak-ing a useful and well-judged contribution to the comprehensive local history being prepared by the adult group.

Certainly a schoolmaster who got himself involved in radical local research of the kind I am suggesting—whether with his own pupils, with interested adults, or with a combination of the two—would not be long before he was introducing relevant local material into his everyday teaching. Moreover, if my own experience is anything to go by, a good deal of it would be material the existence of which he had hardly suspected before.

POSTSCRIPT

O N an earlier page 'community' was inter-preted as "a set of people occupying an area with defined territorial limits and so far united in thought and action as to feel a sense of belonging together, in contradistinction from the many outsiders who do not belong."

The doctrine that local history should concern itself with the life-process of a community in this sense presupposes that the would-be historian will know how to recognize a local community when he sees one on the stage of history. He will have no difficulty with the compact villages of central England or the little market towns, once so tightly knit; but the scattered hamlets of the west or the great urban agglomerations of the nineteenth century may not so patently reveal that "sense of belonging together" which makes them intelligible units of historical study.

It is necessary to insist that locality alone does not provide a suitable or intelligible theme for the historian. I do not know whether Nasser's Egypt is territorially co-extensive with the Egypt of Tutankhamen, but it is obviously not the same community. When Captain Henry Skillicorne founded his spa at Cheltenham he also inaugurated a new local community very different from that of the humdrum market town which preceded it there at the foot of the Cotswold scarp. This is one case —there are many others—where the sense of belonging together has shifted. When it languishes and dies, or is absorbed into some larger loyalty, the history of that particular community is at an end.

Sometimes a new one starts life before its predecessor is quite dead. Manchester is a noted example of a great manufacturing city where the ancient rural manor continued to provide the framework of local government until 1846, by which time the population had risen to nearly a quarter of a million.

Whether the starting-point defines itself, as it does when a community is born on a new site, or has to be discovered amid more complicated beginnings, we are asking the historian to proceed like a landscape artist when he sets out to make a picture of the scene before him. He must delimit it, or in other words decide that just these phenomena, beginning here and ending there, will make a satisfactory picture. It is this part of his function which distinguishes the historian from the antiquary.

Recently, when the doctrine of the "Leicester school" was being debated—and sometimes misrepresented—in the pages of *The Amateur Historian*, a correspondent declared roundly: "Medieval history is not my cup of tea." He evidently did not agree with Ranke that all generations are equal in the sight of God. But a man who is interested only or chiefly in the four or five generations nearest to our own is under no compulsion to attempt the history of a Domesday village, or indeed of any village if his sympathies are predominantly urban.

Another writer complained that to present nineteenth-century history in terms of decline and fall was to give a falsely pessimistic account of a period characterized in fact by abounding optimism. This may well be true: it depends on the local community.

At any given moment in the last hundred and fifty years an ancient village may be rapidly decaying while its population is drawn away to some prosperous new manufacturing centre. History is full of births and deaths.

To the objection that local history as we understand it is too exacting a pursuit for most people, Mr Skipp's observations on team-work supply at least a partial answer.

Finally, the voice of the antiquary is heard asking if there is no room in our scheme of things for one who enjoys collecting facts as other people enjoy collecting prints or china. Indeed there is. We may indulge a hope that he will make his finds accessible to others, and that somebody else will shoulder the task of shaping them into a historical narrative, but with this proviso, let us wish him, with all our heart, good hunting.

H. P. R. FINBERG

INDEX